"An insightful guide full of stories and research to pro.... .... .. the classroom. Cunningham's book about happiness and advocacy for a mind-body connection is more relevant now than ever before!"

—Michael J. Hynes, Superintendent of Schools, Patchogue-Medford School District

"In *Start with Joy*, Katie Cunningham shows readers how you can nourish happiness while still maintaining high literacy standards and getting the results you want—happy students who are readers, writers, and effective communicators. It's a win-win for all."

—Jennifer Allen, author of *Becoming a Literacy Leader,* Second Edition

"This book is beautifully written to help teachers visualize what true student happiness looks, sounds, and feels like. After reading Katie's suggestions, teachers will have a clear pathway for what they can try tomorrow to increase happiness levels. What I love most is that this is not one more thing to fit into the day—it is framed as ways of being with children that can be incorporated into what all teachers are already doing. My hope is that every single student has a teacher who designs with happiness as the main objective and I am grateful that there is now a place to turn to for ideas and support."

—Gravity Goldberg, author of *Teach Like Yourself:
How Authentic Teaching Transforms Our Students and Ourselves*

"This is the book I have been waiting for. Teaching is more than a profession; it is a way of life. Teachers and students alike need to live and learn with greater happiness and joy. With some 'self-literacy' strategies as a key goal in every lesson, Katie shows us how to make connections with our learning and with others in more meaningful ways. I believe that connection is at the heart of happiness, and I believe this book is an invaluable tool to help us achieve it."

—Paula Bourque, author of *Spark: Quick Writes
to Kindle Hearts and Minds in Elementary Classrooms*

"If anyone knows how to cultivate a 'culture of happiness' in the classroom, it's Katie. In *Start with Joy*, she challenges educators to 'prioritize happiness' by embracing the seven main pillars she's developed through her extensive research that, used alongside culturally sustaining practices and attention to students' hearts, minds, *and* bodies, will ultimately lead to more joyful, playful, and purposeful classroom experiences for all."

—Shawna Coppola, author of *Renew: Become a Better
and More Authentic Writing Teacher*

"Katie Cunningham proposes in her new book, *Start with Joy*, that by teaching in ways that value the heart of our humanity—connection, choice, challenge, play, story, discovery, and movement—we pave the pathway to help students become stronger readers and writers. Katie's book offers readers inspired ideas, compelling research, and a treasure trove of rich, carefully selected children's literature recommendations to give us a sensible, refreshing road map for breathing life back into our literacy classrooms."

—Jan Burkins and Kim Yaris, authors of *Who's Doing the Work? How to Say Less So Readers Can Do More*

"In *Start With Joy*, Katie Cunningham draws on a robust body of research to prove that happiness should be cultivated, observed, and reinforced. By reflecting on the stories, accomplishments, and relationships that bring them joy, students can rely on their own resources rather than outside factors in order to feel happy. Finding boundless happiness in her work with children and teachers, she offers a road map for inviting joy into all literacy learning. When building a collection of teacher resources, start with Cunningham!"

—Suzanne Farrell Smith, author of *The Writing Shop: Putting 'Shop' Back in Writing Workshop*

A while ago, a few friends and I discussed what we hoped for in life. After much discussion, we all came to the conclusion that we hope for happiness for ourselves, our loved ones, our students, and each other. So, when I sat down to read *Start with Joy!* I was thrilled! In our increasingly standards-based, testing-focused, stress-inducing school system, happiness is typically neither prioritized nor valued. Enter Katie's beautiful call to action. Katie's Seven Pillars will benefit all teachers and students in all classrooms by bringing the focus back to happiness without sacrificing literacy learning. In fact, her practical suggestions and invitations will enhance literacy learning in classrooms- I know it will in mine! I look forward to turning to this text again and again in my work with both students and teachers.

—Christina Nosek, co-author of *To Know and Nurture a Reader: Conferring with Confidence and Joy*"

Start with JOY

Designing Literacy Learning for Student Happiness

KATIE EGAN CUNNINGHAM

Stenhouse
PUBLISHERS

Portsmouth, New Hampshire

Stenhouse Publishers
www.stenhouse.com

Library of Congress Cataloging-in-Publication Data
Names: Cunningham, Katie Egan, 1978- author.
Title: Start with joy : designing literacy learning for student happiness /
    Katie Egan Cunningham.
Description: Portsmouth, New Hampshire : Stenhouse Publishers, [2019] |
    Summary: "Start with Joy is a guidebook describing ways teachers can make joy and purpose the center of their teaching and students' literacy learning. Organized by seven pillars, based on the science of happiness, this book offers reasons why students' happiness matters now more than ever, providing lessons, strategies, resources, and children's literature suggestions for how to make sure joy and purpose are at the heart of all instruction"—Provided by publisher.
Identifiers: LCCN 2019015441 | ISBN 9781625312839 (paperback) | ISBN
    9781625312846 (ebook)
Subjects: LCSH: Language arts (Elementary) | Motivation in education. | Classroom environment.
Classification: LCC LB1576 .C8546 2019 | DDC 372.6—dc23
LC record available at https://lccn.loc.gov/2019015441

Cover design, interior design, and typesetting by Cindy Butler
Manufactured in the United States of America

PRINTED ON 30% PCW
RECYCLED PAPER

25 24 23 22 21 20 19   9 8 7 6 5 4 3 2 1

*To Jack and Matthew,
you have filled my life with joy.
May we have given you
the roots and the wings
to build a happy life.*

CONTENTS

FOREWORD

I am privileged to write this foreword to such a seminal, important, profound book, written by one of the most inspiring, deeply brilliant literacy leaders I know.

I met Katie years ago when she was a teacher in the classroom, before her years of side-by-side coaching work with teachers, before her masterful leadership at the university level. The very first time we met, her radiance and enormous generosity of spirit were eminently clear and visible to me, and I thought: "How lucky her students are."

We are all lucky now, for Katie has woven her years of experience in the classroom, in the field alongside teachers at all grade levels, and at the university research level to create for us the simplest of all, yet the profoundest of all, messages we can take and use: happiness matters.

The good news about happiness and literacy instruction Katie shares in this book is that they are deeply entwined. The best teaching of reading and writing is the most joyful. The more happiness, joy, and delight we bring into our teaching, the better and more proficient, more empowered our students will be at reading and writing, storytelling, and sharing.

Katie Cunningham is our "happiness guide" in the world of academic learning. In this journey, she shows us how to create a world in which every student is joyfully skillful and skillfully joyful. She shows us how to make it happen in our schools and classrooms, with our students and with all the children and young adults who cross our paths.

Through her careful, research-based, thorough explanation and exploration of connection, choice, challenge, play, story, discovery, and movement, Katie lays out a path and framework for our own powerful literacy instruction through the focus on joy.

And make no mistake, this book will make you feel good professionally and personally, will inspire you, and will bring delight and wonder to your students and your teaching. Its end goal is powerful student engagement and competence in the skills needed to be proficient, confident readers and writers, and along the way, you too will be changed.

To enable us to use her framework, to implement it in our classrooms, and to share it in our schools and districts most effectively, Katie's book is arranged in three parts: the seven pillars of connection, the invitations (actual lessons you can try at any time of the year in the context of any unit), and an appendix of resources to use with your students. Each chapter has powerful, compelling stories, research behind the science and impact of happiness, and many hands-on techniques for you to try in your classroom or to share as an administrative leader or coach across a district large or small.

Choice leads to agency, a feeling of control, which develops into the magical sense of "flow" where we are operating smoothly and easily. Katie supports us in getting to a place of comfort and structure in our teaching, while amplifying guided choice for students and in how we present the lessons, so that we can get into a place of "flow."

From that first day I met Katie, I wanted to work with her, near her, and be inspired by her. In the years that followed, I fulfilled my wish. I saw her and see her changing the lives of teachers, with her humble, generous, invitational spirit. I see her influencing teachers and administrative leaders, coaches and librarians, media specialists, and parents from the ground up: where we are. It feels like magic to work with Katie, and in this book you will have a vibrant, helpful feel for that magic. She embodies herself the often untapped power of happiness. Katie shows us how to bring this superpower into our classrooms and to turn every child, every young adult into a lifelong, skillfully joyful, joyfully skillful reader, writer, and powerful voice in the world.

This book will bring happiness, to you, your teaching, your students, and their learning. Thank you, Katie, for your many gifts, and welcome, teachers, administrators, families, and more, to a hopeful, optimistic world of learning.

Pam Allyn
Founder, LitWorld

ACKNOWLEDGMENTS

In the year of writing this book, my friends and loved ones welcomed new babies into the world, celebrated milestone birthdays, reached new professional heights, and were change agents in their communities. At the same time, friends and loved ones lost their jobs, relocated, mourned family members, fought addiction, and battled cancer. I experienced more joy and heartache than in any other year of my life.

Researching and writing about happiness was a relief in many ways, and at times it was a challenge. Throughout the writing process, I had to ask some hard questions of myself: Could I wholeheartedly practice what I was advocating teachers try in their classrooms with students? Could I maintain a daily gratitude journaling practice and stick with it? Could I go to bed each night and do some honest thinking about whether I had helped make someone else happy? Could I open myself up to new connections when there was no guarantee? Could I share my story as a source of strength? Could I find new ways to play in the classroom and with my own children?

Without a doubt, better understanding the science of happiness has made me a better teacher, mother, partner, and literacy leader. It has made me take notice of the incredible things children do as readers, writers, and communicators that for years may have escaped my attention. It has made me more comfortable with my own strengths and the purpose to my work. It has made the teachers and classes I partner with more joyful, laughter filled, and spontaneous.

As the research shows us, connection is everything. Without the connections, questions, and support of others, this book would not have been possible, and I have many people to thank.

To Maureen, my editor and friend, thank you for your heartfelt check-ins and your patience. You knew exactly the places where children themselves needed to be more present in these pages. This book is better, brighter, and more relevant to teachers thanks to your careful eyes and kind suggestions. If my family has given me roots, you have given me wings. Thank you!

To the Stenhouse family, you have trusted me to create something meaningful for teachers, and I hope I have lived up to what I promised. Dan Tobin, thank you for believing in this work and for welcoming me as a part of the Stenhouse family over the years. It has been life changing to be a part of this professional community of giving, thoughtful people. Thank you, Jay Kilburn, Shannon St. Peter, Lynne Costa, Carly Daubach, Lisa Sullivan and the rest of the editing and production team for imagining how these pages could come to life and marketed. You have brought immeasurable beauty to this work.

To Pam Allyn, thank you for being a mentor and friend this last decade and for contributing your beautiful words through your foreword. You showed me how to be fearless in my beliefs that literacy learning and happiness belong together. Your advocacy that all children have a right to literacy and a right to find happiness is a model of what joyful learning can truly be.

To my teaching friends and soul sisters—Suzanne Farrell Smith, Kristin Rainville, Mary Ann Cappiello, Grace Enriquez, and Erika Dawes. Your ideas about teaching, children's literature, and childhood have influenced my thinking in countless ways. Most of all, your friendship has been an anchor for me as you listened with intention and offered exactly the right kind of support when I needed it most.

To my Manhattanville College colleagues, especially Courtney Kelly, Mary Coakley-Fields, Vicki Fantozzi, Nikki Josephs, and Sherie McClam, thank you for your friendship and for your inspiring research that unpacks what it means to be truly literate in a world that needs people asking questions about sustainability, diversity, and inclusion. Special thanks to Shelley Wepner for her leadership and support over my years at Manhattanville, making my workplace a professional home. My research students at Manhattanville make me a better teacher and thinker. Kelly Garzione deserves special thanks—for your research on accountable talk and for sharing students' authentic responses to stories with me. Thanks to Manhattanville College for granting me a sabbatical, which led to the development and much of the writing of this book.

To the teachers of my own children, especially Lina Rosenberg, Alison Badolato, Carol Maxwell, Erika Racz, Joe Scholz, Brigid Ahern, and Jeff Schwartz, you have made our boys feel like their truest selves each day they were in your care. You supported them with skills and strategies, but, more importantly, Jack and Matthew grew stronger in their sense of belonging and love of learning thanks to you. Lina, thank you for the opportunity to be a part of your classroom and for sharing the spontaneous photos you took throughout the year that captured children working and playing (which were thankfully one and the same).

To the teachers and schools I've been fortunate to partner with, thank you for opening your doors and sharing your classrooms with me. To Dr. Monique Reilly and Veronica Mittzenwei, thank you for saying yes to trying five-minute journaling with your students and seeing what happens. Your classrooms are dynamic, powerful models for others, and I am grateful to learn alongside you.

Missy, Stacey, Caitlyn, Ted, John, Elyse, and The Wooster School, thank you for your willingness to try new things in the name of literacy learning and for the happiness you create for children.

To the children and teachers at Thomas Edison School and Mount Kisco Elementary, especially Matt Casey, Lauren Cutler, Daniella Petrulli, Tracy Cruz, Jennifer Tully, Amy Stern, and Inas Morsi-Hogans, thank you for sharing your children with me. Reading aloud, analyzing student writing, and building classroom libraries gave me new opportunities to admire children.

To the fearless leadership team at Fox Lane Middle School, especially Sue Ostrofsky, Wilma Pabon-Evans, Jason Spector, and Mary Harrison, thank you for the opportunity to think more deeply about the power of discovery in learning by supporting teachers to develop authentic, inquiry-based capstone projects. You have created a school that welcomes new ideas and that empowers teachers to discover alongside children.

To Elaine Natalicchi, Matt Parkin, Martha Hirschman, and the teachers and children from The Dwight School and Dwight London, thank you for opening your classrooms to me as I sought global perspectives on what happiness looks like as a part of learning. You have created school environments driven by discovery of oneself and the world. It's easy to see why the children in your care are smiling, sharing, and skipping through the hallways.

To my mom and dad, Karin and Jim Egan, you give your whole selves to the people you love. There's nothing like a Granny or Gramps. Your love is irreplaceable, and you make our family stronger, kinder, and more hopeful. You taught me that happiness is helping others to live their best lives.

To my sons, Jack and Matthew, thank you for understanding the time I needed to take to write and revise this book. You were the inspiration for these pages and for nearly every decision I've made over the last ten years. You show me what happiness looks like when you ask a rival if they are okay on the soccer field or you help a classmate when you see they need a bit of extra kindness from a friend. Thank you for reminding me that taking the time to play is always a good idea. I cherish our basement sessions of ball tag as much as I do our nightly bedtime reading.

Most of all, thank you to my husband, Chris Cunningham, for modeling what a happy life could be. True to your wild reading heart, you were researching the science of happiness and gently encouraging me to take action in my own life for a long time. You gave me *The Five-Minute Journal* as a Valentine's Day gift, and it was an act of love that changed my life. You opened my eyes to the ways knowledge about happiness could enrich my life and our family. This book and the life we have built would not have been possible without you.

INTRODUCTION

Whether you are a teacher in the early stages of your career or you are a veteran teacher with years of experience, there are always opportunities to make literacy learning for your students more meaningful and memorable. From my years spent as an elementary school teacher and then years observing and coaching teachers, I found there are seven basic pillars that can link what we know from the science of happiness with what we know about effective literacy instruction. These seven pillars will make your classroom more joyful, playful, and purposeful: Connection, Choice, Challenge, Play, Story, Discovery, and Movement. This book is designed to help you master these pillars so that you can support your students to become stronger readers, writers, and communicators while also helping them learn the critical life skills of how to be happy now and for the future.

Have you ever felt like you've taught the "right" lessons, but you wonder whether those lessons mean anything to students? Have you ever felt like the teacher down the hall seemed to have a natural ability to connect with students meaningfully around books and writing in a way that you wished you had? Have you ever laid awake at night thinking about the hopes and dreams you have for your students and how you can better support them to be resilient, compassionate, and self-driven in their own life journey? Have you ever wanted to find a like-minded group of people that also believes that learning how to be happy goes hand in hand with learning how to be a stronger reader, writer, and communicator? Have you ever felt like your teaching needs a jolt of joy to make literacy learning simply more fun? Then this book is for you.

The classrooms I've been fortunate to be a part of and the children I've met have shaped my thinking over the last twenty years about what it means to be truly literate. And now the research from the science of happiness has given us the tools to thoughtfully take action to make the process of becoming a reader, writer, and communicator supportive of the whole child in our care. Over the course of writing this book, I also looked back at my own life and how literacy learning helped me grow roots for my own sustainable happiness starting in childhood.

I have just a few treasures from my childhood I've held on to over the years. One of them is the fourth-grade yearbook that my teacher, Mary Ann Jones, put together for our class. We each wrote a page about ourselves including our favorite songs ("Out of the Blue"—by the '80s legend Debbie Gibson), our favorite sayings ("What a coinkie-dink"), and what we hoped to be when we grew up (a teacher—likely inspired by Mrs. Jones). We were in a basement classroom off in the corner of the school—typical of what sometimes happens to the new teacher in the building. Yet, Mrs. Jones turned our basement corner classroom into something much more, and perhaps the location of our classroom was a blessing that gave her the freedom to try some things that countered literacy instruction of the time. We were encouraged to read voraciously. We made our own decisions about group work. We wrote about our memories. And we made our own yearbooks like we were seniors in high school and signed them for one another. Years later when I taught fourth grade, I replicated the same yearbook project with my students, and I hope some of my students have held on to the things we made together and see them as childhood treasures as I do. Mrs. Jones was only in our school for one year, but she seemed to be ahead of the times in prioritizing our classroom community as a safe space to find happiness while also enriching our literacy lives. What I remember most from that time in my childhood is a sense of security and comfort with myself, which anchored me before the years of adolescence took hold and self-doubt regularly surfaced. I look at the photo of fourth-grade me and I'm grateful for the roots Mrs. Jones gave me that year, which propelled a sense of confidence, courage, and belonging in me.

Over the years of becoming and being a teacher myself, I was fortunate to be a part of many schools. I've taught children who are recent immigrants and who take care of their younger siblings after school, changing diapers and making bottles when their parents are at work. I've also taught children who experience enormous economic privilege but wrote in their notebooks about feeling lonely at home. I've taught children from all backgrounds who arrive early and stay late, seeking a place to feel belonging and connection. In every school I have been a part of, I have tried to discover everything I could about what makes children thrive in their learning. I've asked questions. I've read widely. I've planned. And I've tried new methods. All to deepen my understanding about the childhood roots of lifelong happiness and where that naturally intersects with the

Me in Childhood

ways we organize, plan, and teach literacy. The more time I spent in other people's classrooms as a coach, the more I began to notice the common threads across classrooms where children seemed happy in their learning. Often, this was the result of small, intentional shifts to focus more on joy as a fundamental catalyst for learning. Meanwhile, society at large has seen an explosion of interest in happiness with science now supporting what has seemed like common sense.

No longer a mystery, the seven pillars explored through this book will help you prioritize happiness as an integral part of your literacy instruction. These seven pillars have become a mental checklist for me every time I walk into a classroom: Connection, Choice, Challenge, Play, Story, Discovery, and Movement. Where do I see it? Where can there be more of it? What are the steps to get there? Over the last few years, my pursuit for seeing what happiness looks like as a part of literacy learning took me back to schools where I began my teaching journey in New York. From there, I visited schools in London and partnered with Kenyan teachers. Stepping outside American classrooms gave me a chance to see and learn about what matters most to teachers in other parts of the world. I saw teachers playing ping-pong with students during recess. Children led me around their school gardens and talked about what brought them joy at school. Teachers shared what was in their hearts. Children left me with hugs. I returned home and was more committed than ever to make happiness less of a mystery and more of a tangible reality for all children in any circumstance as a part of literacy learning.

When I've presented these pillars or I've modeled the practices described in this book, without exception, I have heard from teachers and school leaders that this focus on happiness is the work they want to do for their school community. We know happiness can predict health and longevity. Happiness scales are even being used to measure social progress. Yet, happiness isn't something that just happens to you. Happiness can grow when we make small changes to our own behavior, mindset, and relationships. Twenty years after my journey as a teacher began and over thirty years since my fourth-grade self envisioned a meaningful life as a teacher, I feel more hopeful that a focus on happiness can become as much a priority in our planning and our teaching as skills and strategies have rightfully become.

I hope this book will change the way you think about teaching and learning. That you feel more hopeful. More purposeful. More in awe of your students. More knowledgeable about books and stories. More connected to children. More driven to prioritize happiness. More joyful.

HOW TO USE THIS BOOK

This book is composed of three parts: the pillars, the invitations, and an appendix of resources. I recommend that you begin at the beginning and read it straight through to the end. But, you can also jump to the pillars that intrigue you the most. Each chapter has stories, research behind the science of happiness, and many techniques for you to try in your own classroom. Come back to chapters later that feel most relevant to you and your students. Readers new to teaching will quickly catch on to the pillars and why they are important. More experienced teachers will find something new to try in every chapter that can bring energy and enthusiasm for literacy learning into your classroom. Hopefully you find "aha!" tidbits that you immediately want to try.

The second part of the book has ten "invitations." These are lessons that you can try at any time of year in the context of any unit. There are children's literature suggestions and sample teacher talk to help you try an invitation that fits the needs of your class right away. But like any invitation, these lessons are designed for you to improvise and make your own.

Finally, there is an appendix with some tools to help your students tell their story and make literacy learning a time of the day that all students look forward to. Most of all, I hope this book helps you think about your own ways of intentionally teaching toward happiness as a part of literacy learning. Although happiness is about much more than pleasure (the rest of the book will explain), I hope you enjoy the pleasure of reading this book. Light a candle. Pour a cup of tea. Try something new. Have some fun with it. Start with joy.

Chapter 1

Why Happiness?
Why Now?

> The noblest art is that of making others happy.
>
> —P. T. Barnum

At the end of A. A. Milne's (1928) beloved classic, *The House at Pooh Corner*, Christopher Robin has a heartfelt exchange with his dearest friend as he says goodbye to Pooh and, essentially, to childhood itself:

> "I'm not going to do Nothing any more."
>
> "Never again?"
>
> "Well, not so much. They don't let you."
>
> Pooh waited for him to go on, but he was silent again.
>
> "Yes, Christopher Robin," said Pooh helpfully.
>
> "Pooh, when I'm—you know—when I'm not doing
>
> Nothing, will you come up here sometimes?"
>
> "Just me?"
>
> "Yes, Pooh."
>
> "Will you be here too?"
>
> "Yes, Pooh, I will be, really. I promise I will be, Pooh."
>
> "That's good," said Pooh.
>
> "Pooh, promise me you won't forget about me, ever.
>
> Not even when I'm a hundred."
>
> Pooh thought for a little.
>
> "How old shall I be then?"
>
> "Ninety-nine."

Pooh nodded.

"I promise," he said.

Still with his eyes on the world Christopher Robin put

out a hand and felt for Pooh's paw.

"Pooh," said Christopher Robin earnestly, "if I—if

I'm not quite—" he stopped and tried again—"Pooh,

whatever happens, you will understand, won't you?"

"Understand what?"

"Oh, nothing." He laughed and jumped to his feet.

"Come on!"

"Where?" said Pooh.

"Anywhere," said Christopher Robin.

Milne reminds us that children often know what brings them the greatest joy—companionship from a true friend, the freedom to make choices about their time, and a sense of possibility. He also subtly reminds us that childhood is fleeting, inestimable, and worthy of deep, intentional care.

When September arrives, we know that the Christopher Robins of our classrooms are in our trust for a limited amount of time each day and year. We mark the hundredth day of school because it's a reminder that the class has reached a milestone together and that the school year is curving toward completion. Before our eyes, children grow out of their clothing and into new friendships. They lose teeth and get scrapes. They fall down and get back up again. They try new things and set their own goals. They imagine worlds in their minds and tell stories to themselves. They gain new skills, ask thought-provoking questions, and apply new strategies. We hope they will find books that they fall in love with and characters they admire. All of this happens almost by magic. Most importantly, the roots of their happiness begin to take shape.

WHAT DO YOU REALLY WANT FOR YOUR STUDENTS?

This book is written with the assumption that children go to school each day to become stronger readers, writers, and thinkers, yes . . . but equally important, they walk into school and hope to be happy. Think of your own students. Picture their faces in your mind. When you see them smiling, what are they doing? How do you know when they are happy? Then, think to yourself, *What do I really want for my students?* On some days, you may respond that you want them all to be confident, fluent readers or that you want them to find their voice as writers. On other days, you may want them to find books and authors they fall in love with so that they read and keep reading. These are worthy and important goals. But if you consider the question long enough, your reply will likely include one particular word: *happy*. If we take certain steps, we can support students to be successful readers, writers, and communicators while also greatly increasing the chances that they will find joy in learning, and more importantly, that they will be laying the foundation for sustained happiness that they can learn to keep creating for themselves their entire lives.

LOOKING AND LISTENING FOR HAPPINESS

This book is designed as a guide to help you put your students' happiness at the center of learning without sacrificing the literacy goals you are striving to support your students to achieve. I'm a person who mostly looks and listens for a living. I look and listen for strength, wisdom, and joy in schools. In my school visits, I get to witness extraordinary teachers and school leaders that support the children in their care to not only learn but to find joy in their learning. I meet teachers like Missy, whose kindergarten classroom is driven by a spirit of experimentation. Missy started to realize that some of her students were entering kindergarten already with pressures to read. So, Missy and I partnered to rethink how to launch the school year to make joy the top priority in her literacy instruction from Day One. When I shared with Missy the interactive picture book *Say Zoop!* by Hervé Tullet (2017), she leapt at the chance to try it out with her students. Tullet's interactive picture books are visually stunning and invite readers to play through a series of simple, colored dots. By following instructions like "whisper oh" and "shout OH," readers participate in the reading process by making their voices match the size and shape of the dots. Together, Missy and I decided it would be joyful and purposeful to start guided reading in the fall with Tullet's interactive picture books instead of starting with leveled books. We found that the magic of Tullet's books created a feeling of joy and a zest for reading that we could never muster through our enthusiasm alone. Setting the tone for guided reading for the year with a book as mystifying as *Say Zoop!* made every student eager for the next guided reading session. As their voices responded to the changing dots with *oh*s and *OH*s, they were engaging in the cognitive work that reading print demands. At the same time, the roots for a year of happiness through literacy learning were being formed. Leveled books came later, but joy came first.

I also meet people like Ted, a third-grade teacher, who begins the school year getting to know every student by finding out about their likes, dislikes, pets, hobbies, hopes, fears, and challenges. Ted is the kind of teacher that his former students gravitate toward because they know he is always available to listen or offer a word of encouragement. One of the first read-alouds Ted does every year is B. J. Novak's (2014) *The Book With No Pictures*, which introduces his students to the idea that the written word holds a lot of power, that words can be nonsensical, and that words can even be a source of mischief. As Ted reads, the lines of text are designed to ignite collective laughter, and the children begin to learn that this is a classroom where laughter is valued and, in fact, expected.

Missy and Ted recognize that teaching and learning must be driven by joy and purpose. They respond intentionally when learning feels dispirited or they see their class becoming overly stressed. And they recognize that the process of meeting literacy goals must also be a process that intentionally supports student happiness. Their most trusted method for doing so is to turn to books they know invite students into the learning. They know their students don't want to be taught at; they want to be a part of.

SOME BURNING QUESTIONS

Both in schools and in the general public, we are in the midst of a cultural and scientific revolution. There is a growing interest in the study of happiness and what it means for people of all ages. Books with eye-catching titles like *Flourish* (Seligman 2012), *Drive* (Pink 2009), *Presence* (Cuddy 2015), *Quiet* (Cain 2012), *Mindset* (Dweck 2006), and *Grit* (Duckworth 2016) all explore the factors that influence performance but also sustained happiness. The last decade has seen an explosion of interest in the field of positive psychology, and educators have instituted growth mindset curricula in the hopes of increasing children's capacities to learn, grow, and persevere. Schools have thoughtfully embedded mindset language and exercises for students to be more optimistic, empathetic, and flexible. Classrooms across the country have instituted brain breaks through engaging videos that prompt children to mimic movements for bursts of physical activity to optimize subsequent thinking. Meditation is becoming increasingly common especially through kid-friendly apps like Headspace. All of this is valuable and important. Yet, when I observe children in school, I wonder what is still missing for many of them to see school as a place consistently driven by and supportive of their happiness.

In her book *Better Than Before*, Gretchen Rubin (2013) writes, "I spend most of my time trying to grasp the obvious—not to see what no one has seen, but to see what's in plain sight" (3). The diminishing of children's sustained happiness in school started to feel to me like something that's in plain sight. So I started to ask myself some questions:

- What is happiness? What does it look like in school? What does it look like in literacy learning?
- In what ways can we make our classrooms more joyful by tapping into students' hearts and bodies as much as their minds?
- How can we intentionally plan for students' happiness as well as their understanding? In other words, how can we design our way there?

This book attempts to answer these questions and to give you practical ways to cultivate a culture of happiness in your classroom through an integrated approach to literacy teaching and learning by honoring children's hearts and bodies as much as their minds. This book is also my response to noticing happiness and life design courses becoming increasingly popular at elite universities including Harvard, Yale, University of Pennsylvania, and Stanford. The tenets of these courses and the research from these institutions on happiness and well-being have profoundly shaped my thinking and public discourse. Yet, I started to wonder why the strategies that lead to sustained happiness require an Ivy League education. I wanted to take the research on happiness and embed it as a part of literacy learning starting with our youngest elementary school students because all children deserve the possibility of applying happiness techniques to their lives. Literacy instruction as a learning block grounded by stories, sharing, community, and reflection seemed to me the natural instructional space for teachers to integrate happiness techniques.

This book is designed so that you can try new methods and see immediate changes in yourself and your students. In this book, I utilize the concept of an "invitation" as an opportunity to try something with your students. When we receive an invitation in the mail, we immediately feel a sense that we are important at least to the person that sent it. In our classrooms, we can use an "invitations" approach to support students to feel as though they have agency in their own learning process. An invitation is not forced. It is not a requirement. The invitations shared in this book do not replace strategy instruction that has a critical role in literacy instruction. Rather, these invitations complement those strategies to boost student happiness and performance in sustainable ways.

The source of the word *happiness* is the Icelandic word *happ*, which means "luck" or "chance." It's the same root for the words *haphazard* and *happenstance*. Yet, children's happiness cannot be left to chance but rather should be ensured *by design*. As a field, we have been focused on designing instruction for student understanding for decades. Isn't it time we designed our instruction for student happiness as well?

IF NOT NOW, WHEN?

In 1928, A. A. Milne knew that childhood is a sacred time in its own right. Today, the need for childhood itself to be honored and valued is increasingly urgent. Psychology researcher Peter Gray (2010) explains, "We would like to think of history as progress, but if progress is measured in the mental health and happiness of young people, then we have been going backward at least since the early 1950s." Several key indicators support Gray's claim.

Partner Story Planning

According to UNICEF (2007), the children of the United States are the second *least* happy children in the world as detailed in the UNICEF Report Card on children's well-being in the twenty-nine wealthiest countries. Rates of depression are ten times higher today than they were in the 1960s, and the average age for the onset of depression is fourteen and a half compared with twenty-nine and a half in 1960 (Gray 2010). According to the Institute for Research and Reform in Education, as many as 60 percent of America's children feel chronically disengaged from school whether they live in urban, suburban, or rural settings (Klem and Connell 2004). In one study, 61 percent of fourth graders agreed with the statement, "I am happy with my life." By seventh grade, only 36 percent made the same claim (Klem and Connell 2004).

David Elkind (2007) author of *The Power of Play: How Spontaneous, Imaginative Activities Lead to Happier, Healthier Children*, offers further startling statistics about the urgency of childhood today. He writes, "At the first ever Surgeon General's Conference on Children's Mental Health in 2000, it was reported that 'growing numbers of children are suffering needlessly because their emotional, behavioral and developmental needs are not being met by the very institutions that were explicitly created to take care of them.' This may be the first generation of American children who are less healthy than their parents" (x). One such institution is school.

As these and other startling statistics are shared, the need for social-emotional learning in school is getting increased attention. Yet it is often parceled off as something separate from academic instruction. How we cope day to day with our thoughts, feelings, emotions, and connections to others informs what and how we read, write, listen, and speak. A strong social-emotional self is part of having a strong literacy self. A primary goal of becoming a strong reader and writer is to help one design the life they want to lead. A happy life.

What does a happy life look like? It may look different for each of us but there are some common threads that researchers have found from longitudinal studies. A happy life is associated with feelings of meaning and purpose. A happy life is one where compassion, generosity, and love abound. A happy life is filled with opportunities to feel a sense of accomplishment, taking healthy risks (and succeeding), and failing and trying again. A happy life is one where other people matter.

HAPPINESS IN YOUR OWN HEART

Think about your own happiness and where it comes from. Who are the people you love? What are the places you love? What are the things you do that make you happy? What are the small things in life you notice that make you happy?

Turn to a fresh page in a journal or create a new Google Doc and create your own happiness list. Jot whatever comes to mind. It will reaffirm for you the enormous worth in your own life.

Here are some of my jottings when I think of what makes me happy:

1. The sound of Chris, my husband, playing a new song on his ukulele

2. Watching my son, Matthew, climb on boulders in our backyard while acting out stories

3. Talking to my son, Jack, before bed about his day

4. Reading a book with characters I fall in love with

5. The feeling of my "blanket scarf," a gift from my mom, around my neck

6. Getting a fire going by myself on a winter morning

7. Sitting in the 4:00 sun in the summertime

8. The smell of clementines being peeled

9. Listening to my dad's voice on a video he's taken of one of my boys

10. The sound of laughter coming from anyone anytime

My list is about connections and feelings that are basically simple—the people I love being their truest selves, moments of independence and success, being more connected to nature, feeling as though my life has purpose, and that I am needed by others. By listing what makes you happy, you are more able to be wide awake or mindful of what makes you happy. Did you notice that the act of listing what makes you happy immediately makes you happier? You turn your attention more automatically to the sensations that bring sustained happiness. I recommend starting a list and adding to it when it occurs to you or at a set time in your schedule. A simple place to start this in your classroom is by giving students an opportunity to generate their own happiness lists with reminders at set times in the week to add to their list new things they noticed that made them happy. Building this into a classroom routine helps students visualize the people, places, and moments that make them happy as a habit. In doing so, they can start to learn that they have the power to channel their own happiness, and that in doing so, they can help others grow in their happiness, too.

WHAT WE KNOW ABOUT HAPPINESS AND LEARNING

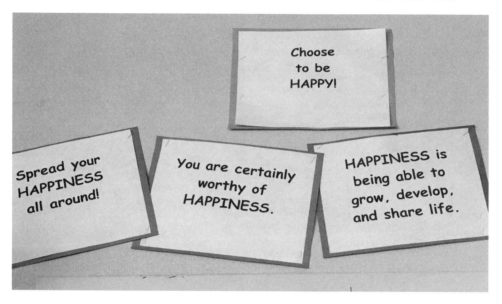

People, everywhere and always, have sought the key to happiness. Aristotle declared happiness to be *summum bonum*, the chief good. Over 2000 years later, the quest for the chief good continues. Yet, what's new is the growing body of scientific research on what actually makes people happy—and a sense from teachers, administrators, families, and researchers that today's children are particularly vulnerable when it comes to finding sustained happiness.

When you watch children climbing the steps onto their school bus or walking through the front door of school, they are hoping to have an emotionally enriching and balanced day. Children expect and want well-being at school. They want to be socially connected, to discover new things, and to feel successful thanks to their own efforts. They want to find their purpose.

When you look out into your classroom, what is the emotional temperature of your students? What do you look for? Maybe you look for signs of student engagement like students looking and listening to speakers. Hands in the air. Question posing. You are probably looking for the ways your students feel supported by you and by their peers and by their willingness to ask for help when they need it. You may be noticing the ways that the lesson feels relevant to students and their lives through the ways they talk about what they are learning. Yet, how many of us stop to look for happiness?

Jessica Lahey, a middle school English teacher and author of *The Gift of Failure* (2015), wrote an article for the *New York Times* titled, "Letting Happiness Flourish in the Classroom" (2016). In the article she explains her process of looking for happiness in her classroom: "I stopped looking for happiness long ago. I see it periodically, when the conditions are perfect, and the stars align just so. When happiness strikes in my classroom, I relish it as I would any other rare anomaly, like thundersnow, or a two-faced calf." I think most of us feel like Lahey when we think about happiness as a priority, especially when faced with an onslaught of new initiatives. So, what does it take for happiness to be a regular sighting, not by chance but by design?

Researchers are looking at happiness in new ways and are finding that emotions are closely related to cognitive, behavioral, motivational, and physiological processes and are also critical for learning and achievement. Dr. Emma Seppala (2017) is the author of *The Happiness Track* and Science Director of Stanford's Center for Compassion and Altruism Research and Education. She has found that happy kids show up at school more able to learn because they tend to sleep better and may have healthier immune systems. Seppala explains in the *Times* piece by Lahey, "Happiness is not something we can afford to lose at home or in our classrooms, as it forms the very foundation of deep, meaningful learning." She further explains, "Happy kids learn faster and think more creatively. Happy kids tend to be more resilient in the face of failures. Happy kids have stronger relationships and make new friends more easily." Seppala also cautions that we put our children's happiness at risk when we model the "*myths of success*: the belief that success is inextricably tied to stress and anxiety, perseverance at all costs, avoidance of personal weakness, and a myopic focus on cultivating expertise in a specialized niche."

So how can we counter this myth of success in our literacy teaching? We can emphasize strengths while also acknowledging that we all face challenges. We can recognize the signs that learning has become stressful and anxiety producing, and we can counter that by modeling positivity. We can turn to characters that live complex lives but who find happiness by helping others. We can follow up by asking our students every day: "What did you do today that made someone else happy?"

We sometimes assume as educators that students will be happy, engaged, and well behaved in school after they've achieved some academic goals. Yet, the skills of happiness and positivity can actually be taught first with the understanding that positive emotions are not simply a phenomenon to enjoy after we have achieved something but are tools we can use to increase our chances of achieving something significant. There are practical ways to foster well-being including the following:

- Develop a positive student/teacher relationship with each student.
- Engage students with relevant, interesting, and compelling lessons.
- Help students identify their strengths—specifically, look for strengths in past experiences, and discuss how to use them in future learning.
- Make students feel special while avoiding empty praise.
- Cultivate hope and optimism by reminding students of previous success from hard work.

These are suggestions we have heard before for good reason. Research reminding us of the benefits of happiness keeps piling up. In many ways, I witness classrooms trying these suggested techniques here and there. But there remains a need to have rituals and routines in place to integrate these techniques into learning itself rather than for them to remain separate. When happiness is seen as something separate from learning, it becomes the first thing to be squeezed out, becoming as regular as thundersnow or the two-faced calf that Lahey describes.

Children are really our best experts on happiness. When we ask kids about what makes them happy and what would make them happier at school, they have simple but profound responses. I often pose to children in schools and in my own life the questions "What makes you happy at school, and what would make you happier at school?" The answers are as varied as children themselves. Some children want more time to read and draw. Not to practice a particular strategy or skill, but simply to read and draw. Other children respond with the hopes of hands-on opportunities like more building time. A frequent response from both boys and girls is the need for more movement and less time sitting on a classroom rug. Many children respond that they want more time outdoors. My oldest son, Jack, responded, "Mom, school would be more fun if we could just talk sometimes and if we were allowed to laugh." It would be a mistake to assume one certain method, activity, or technique would be best for all children.

Some children will show us through their actions and their words when they find learning joyful. At one of the schools I partner with, I lead an afterschool "litclub" of third, fourth, and fifth graders. All of the children are bilingual learners, and many of them are recent immigrants. The school is located in an area where children are sometimes transient and where food insecurity is a significant challenge. Many of the children live with a single parent, grandparent, or other relative. Our litclub promotes an atmosphere driven by stories, collaboration, and choice.

On the first day I read aloud Eileen Spinelli's (2008) *The Best Story* and ask the children what they think the best story is and whether they agree with the characters. One year, a fourth-grade boy named Angel talked back to the text throughout the read-aloud—"That's not the best story." He lay down on the rug and then finally walked away from our circle. He was still figuring out whether he could trust this litclub or whether he could trust me and the others in the group. But as soon as we turned to a discussion of the kinds of promises we could make to one another as members of a litclub, Angel had the first suggestion. He hoped we could have share time when anyone can share something that's on their mind or something they've brought in. After that first afternoon, Angel was the first student to arrive and the last to leave every week for two years. He led our share time and frequently told stories from his life, especially about living with his cousins. He shared his prized Pokemon cards, his comic drawings, and his anime hand-drawn cutout creations. Acknowledging his request for share time was simple. I could have misunderstood Angel entirely in that first read-aloud. I could have chastised him for calling out. I could have seen his departure from our circle as rude. I could have dismissed him from our litclub entirely. I'm grateful that I saw his disruption as fear of the unknown and not as a personal attack. With a little space and the invitation to return and shape our litclub time together, Angel became our strongest contributor. With commitments to one another in place, learning soared. Children read stories, poems, and news articles. They wrote their own narratives and comic books. They created Shadow Puppet digital stories and acted out scripts they wrote themselves. Striving to create a foundation in happiness rooted in understanding of every student can help create the conditions for deep, meaningful learning.

  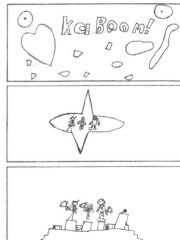

Partner Comic Writing

SELF-LITERACY AS A FUNDAMENTAL GOAL OF LITERACY LEARNING

For decades we have been teaching literacy strategies based on what we know about proficient readers and writers. This is important work. Yet, when we reconceptualize literacy strategies as life strategies, then self-literacy, or better understanding yourself, becomes a key goal of every literacy lesson. Self-literacy is the knowledge of your body and your mind and how the two work together to support your thoughts, emotions, movements, and health. Self-literacy is power. It's nothing short of a miracle that we wake up every morning and our bodies know how to keep our heart beating, our lungs breathing, and our brain working. But we all wake up and experience life differently. When you know yourself, you feel stronger at everything—school, work, sports, friendships, life. When students understand themselves, they can make their way through the world with a deeper knowledge of who they are, who they will be, and how they connect to others in meaningful ways.

Veronica and Monique teach fourth grade in a Title I school outside New York City. Their students are culturally, linguistically, and economically diverse. Some of their students experience homelessness. There are several newcomer students in each of their classrooms learning English for the first time. Nearly one-fourth of their students have special ed intervention. When you walk into Veronica's and Monique's classrooms, you see thoughtful instruction, students working in partnerships, and diverse classroom libraries. When I approach children about what they are working on, they say things like "I'm working on my goal as a writer to really grab my reader. I've decided to use a question." and "I'm helping my classmate use Google Translate to help her figure out these directions." Children are what you might think of as engaged. They have a strong sense of purpose around learning and helping others.

Veronica and Monique wanted to partner with me to explicitly focus on happiness because year after year they witnessed anxiety, stress, and insecurity increase for their students leading up to and during testing season. Veronica and Monique wanted to try something that would be a simple routine that wouldn't take much class time that the students could ultimately take ownership of each day. We decided to introduce the students to a new five-minute journaling routine. Every day as part of their morning routine, students jotted in their journals responses to the same three prompts:

I am grateful for _____ .

What would make today great?

I am _____ .

Then at the end of the school day before dismissal, they jotted down two more responses to the prompts:

_____ was amazing today.

Something I learned today _____ .

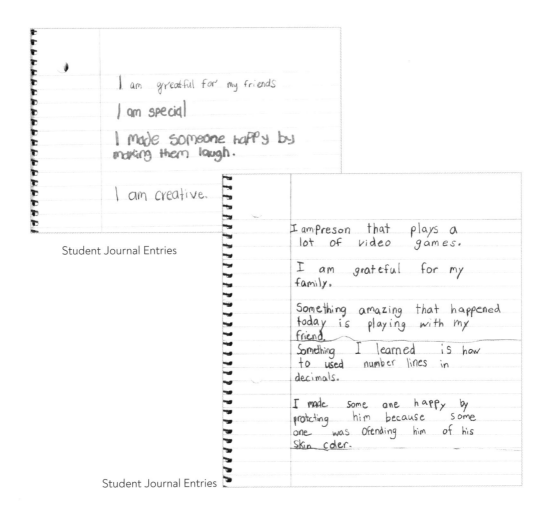

I am greatful for my friends

I am special

I made someone happy by making them laugh.

I am creative.

Student Journal Entries

I am preson that plays a lot of video games.

I am grateful for my family.

Something amazing that happened today is playing with my friend.

Something I learned is how to used number lines in decimals.

I made some one happy by protcting him because some one was ofending him of his skin coler.

Student Journal Entries

I'am a prinhces.

I am gratefal for cleqn the haus.

Something amazing that hqappened today ip. pan Keits with nutela.

Something I learned today is multoplyke shoh.

10/4   Something amazing that happened today is y went homi my mom bru a sand Kasd

I made semeone else happy today by I given my mom a hog and a Kis

Student Journal Entries

Before the journaling project began, we asked students to complete a short survey to gauge their gratitude about school, their friends and family, their feelings about learning, and how much agency they felt they had in their day. After only one month (twenty days) of journaling, we administered the same survey. In that short time, we found that most students looked forward to school more; felt more proud of themselves; felt more gratitude toward friends, family, and school; and had a greater sense of agency about their attitudes and actions such as their willingness to ask a question and their willingness to try something difficult again. With just five minutes a day and twenty days of the same journaling routine, we were starting to impact children's mindsets to recognize the sources of their own happiness. This is consistent with research on habit formation that shows us that it takes twenty days to change your habits for the long term. As Will Durant (paraphrasing Aristotle) wrote,

"We are what we repeatedly do" (not what we do once in a while) (1926, 87). Additionally, the act of writing down their short responses was critical to the process. To write something down is to make it tangible. To make it known. To commit. Literacy was integral to their happiness development.

When we looked at their journal responses, we started to take notice of the most common responses, but we also took note of things that surprised us. The most common things students were grateful for were not surprising: their friends, family, mom, teachers, having a home, dad, pets, and body. But their gratitude statements also included things like "I am grateful when people respect me" and "I am grateful for making other kids laugh." These responses showed the understanding that these fourth graders had that making others happy is the greatest source of finding sustained happiness in our own lives. Research shows they're right.

Perhaps most revealing of all were their "I Am" statements that were as varied as they are. The most common "I Am" statements were: "I am strong"; "I am smart"; "I am grateful"; and "I am a good friend." We found their responses uplifting and affirming in many ways. The journaling process helped students recognize the good inside of them especially with statements like: "I am a miracle"; "I am trying my best"; "I am ready for anything." But students also used this as a space to write things that gave us great pause including: "I am trying not to talk" and "I can make it through the day." When fourth graders authentically reflect that they are trying to make it through the day, there is work to be done to give all students a foundation in the life strategies that can help build a happy life. Literacy learning is a natural pathway to get there.

Strategically and intentionally supporting students to write down their thoughts in this way did not require a big time commitment. It was five minute each day. It did require a belief that daily writing could be a path toward student happiness. It required a commitment to the journaling practice knowing that it could support students with the kind of self-literacy that can lead to sustained happiness.

When I've shared this five-minute journaling technique with teachers around the country, they've sent me back their students' responses: "I am grateful for my dog, Gussie Wussie"; "Something that would make today great would be if the sun came out"; "Something that would make today great would be if I got to talk to my cousins"; "I am courageous and daring." One teacher shared with me that she noticed one girl wrote "I am sad" three days in a row and thanks to the five-minute journaling practice, she knew she needed to approach her to offer help. She also bravely raised the question: But, why haven't I helped *yet*? The technique is simple, but the results are profound.

There are other researchers and practitioners engaging in the wholehearted work of linking literacy learning with learning about life. Dr. Martin Seligman, one of the first and leading voices of positive psychology, studied eight classes of middle school students who read *Lord of the Flies* (Golding 1954) and other novels for a literature course. They were then randomly assigned to two groups: one group took eighty-minute classes on kindness and other topics that related to the books and was asked to do three kind deeds in their communities, while the other was given no positive psychology training. Two years later, Seligman, along with other colleagues, looked at how the students who took a year of literature courses infused with positive psychology compared with peers who had literature alone and found a significant difference in their school performance. The courses that incorporated elements of positive psychology linked the literature they were reading to actions students could take in their own lives to focus on the happiness of others. The results showed that the application of positive psychology lessons stuck with the students over time. New habits and mindsets had been formed. Seligman explains, "The kids who had the positive psychology literature courses were rated by their teacher as having higher social skills. Their zest for learning is higher and their grades are better." The results in many ways replicated what Veronica, Monique, and I found in our study of their fourth graders—that we can design experiences for students that link literacy experiences with sustained, student happiness.

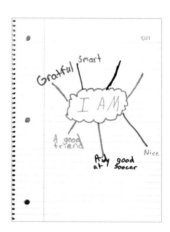

Our classrooms can create opportunities for students to notice what they think, how they act, and how they feel about themselves and to bravely share those noticings as a part of literacy learning. For example, at the start of the school year we can ask students to write, draw, and share things like:

"I Am" Brainstorms

- What three words best describe you?
- What is unique about you that leads to your happiest times?
- What are your strengths, and how can you use them?

When I asked these questions to students in my afterschool litclub, I heard from Monika that "my strengths are my confidence and my risk-taking in meeting new people." Monika was new to the school that year, but you would never know that looking at her ease with others in the group, especially when it came time to share what books they loved. Dayana told our group that her strength was something we couldn't see but that was always a part of her—her heart. Lester and Alan opened their notebooks and decided to make "I Am" brainstorm maps that listed words that they felt best described them.

When we give students a chance to self-reflect, we can then leverage this self-recognition by asking the same questions about characters to help deepen students' understanding of stories. This sparks closer reading, deeper thinking, and more stamina, which are skills we all strive for in our literacy teaching. After writing their own "I Am" brainstorms, Lester and Alan then applied the same thinking to the characters Square and Triangle from the eponymous books by Mac Barnett and Jon Klassen (2017, 2018). This in turn led them to write their own shape stories modeled after Square and Triangle ("Oval and Diamond") with characters that had equally unique qualities. In reading the boys' "Oval and Diamond" story, you can see the ways that they show readers that friendship is complicated and sometimes thinking of someone else's happiness first can lead to finding your own happiness.

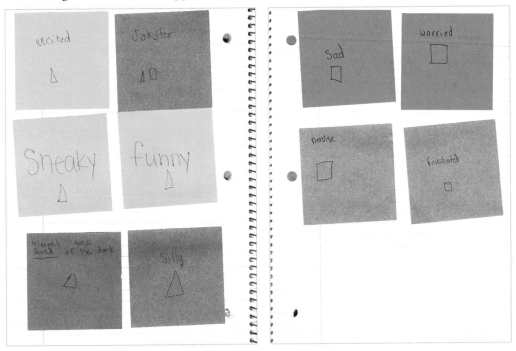

Jotting Character Traits

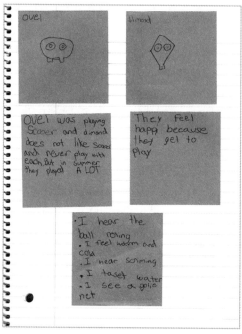

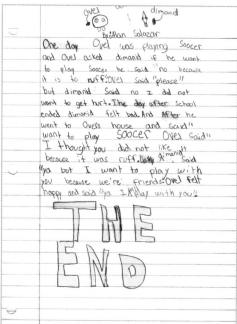

"Oval and Diamond" Story Plan and Writing Based on Mac Barnett and
Jon Klassen's Books *Triangle* and *Square*

In addition to considering their own strengths and the strengths of characters, what if students were supported to notice and pay attention to when they are enjoying what they are doing in school and when they are bored? Or when they are happy and when they are frustrated? Or when they are interested and when they are confused? To simply experience and honor these feelings and reactions and then to note them? That would be self-literacy and metacognition at its highest and most important level—to be aware of your own thought process about yourself and to be aware of the things you love.

What does this look like in the context of literacy teaching and learning? In addition to focusing on recognizing patterns in text, students can also recognize patterns in themselves. Although we have long advocated for readers to find authors, genres, and series that shape their reading identities, perhaps we can do more to support students to acknowledge how their reading is changing their thinking about themselves or others. At the end of every guided reading lesson, what if we asked students, "What made you feel strong today as a reader?" What if we had students high-five their neighbor after independent reading for a job well done? What if when they thought they did something amazing as readers, kids were encouraged to do a power pose that allowed their bodies to shape their minds? What if after a character-driven read-aloud, students created drawings of what was in the character's heart as well as their own? The possibilities for self-literacy connections are a major emphasis of the framing of this book and the invitations presented.

HAPPINESS AND BECOMING A READER AND WRITER

Linking literacy learning with what we know from the science of happiness is possible. Looking globally can help. In July 2018, the Dalai Lama launched a happiness curriculum for over 800,000 children in Delhi's Government Schools, pioneering a much-needed response to promote children's mental well-being. Why? India has one of the highest teen suicide rates. This happiness curriculum is aimed at an education for the heart as much as an education for the mind and includes meditation, mental exercises, and powerful narratives for students to interpret and discuss. This may be the beginning of a global revolution in education to make students' well-being and the fulfillment of their emotions as important as academic achievement. The pathway to get there is through stories, reflection, and discussion—all critical literacy engagements we can design instruction around.

Yet, in addition to designing curriculum that intentionally embeds stories, reflection, and discussion (all explored more in the pillars to come), we can also change how we give feedback to students based on what we know from the science of happiness. After all, learning to read and learning to write are actually quite hard. A lot of repetition, practice, and hard work goes into growing our brains as readers and writers. The good news is that our goals of supporting students to grow in their skills and strategies as readers, writers, and communicators can support our goals of helping students grow in their happiness. We want students to be fluent, proficient, self-driven readers. We also want students to find joy now and to develop the roots in childhood of adult happiness. These four simple steps can be used to start bridging literacy instruction with intentional happiness using whatever curriculum might be guiding your instruction by focusing on how you give feedback to students:

- **Step One: Small Moments of Joy**—focus on noticing and naming small moments of joy.
- **Step Two: Look Forward to Practice**—help students look forward to the practice necessary to get good at anything, especially things they care about and are interested in.
- **Step Three: Mastery Comes from Effort**—support students to feel a sense of mastery that comes from effort.
- **Step Four: Positive Recognition**—provide ways for students to garner recognition from their peers and teachers.

What does that look like in practice? Manny is a first-grade reader who is described by his teacher as persistent. He is a social member of the class and enjoys working in reading partnerships. He has worked hard all year to focus during word study instruction so that he now applies his phonics knowledge to read words with greater accuracy and automaticity. He has started to take home books from the Fly Guy series (Arnold 2005) because he thinks they're funny and because he also knows they are books that challenge him to attend to print. Reading assessments show that Manny's reading behaviors are strongly associated with using meaning and syntax cues, and he is working on attending to print and applying strategies to figure out unknown words. This is hard work for a first grader when vowel patterns they may not have learned yet start to appear in books. Manny has a teacher who knows a great deal about how she can support her students to find joy in the process of becoming a stronger reader and writer. Here are some of the ways she has focused on applying the science of happiness into her conferences with Manny:

Small Moments of Joy	Look Forward to Practice	Mastery Comes from Effort	Positive Recognition
Manny, you are working hard as a reader. What are some of the things that made you smile while you were reading today? . . . That sounds like a small moment of joy.	You have really been practicing and practicing to focus on the letters in each word. It takes a lot of practice to get good at things. What are you looking forward to practicing next?	Wow, you really zoomed in on the letters in the word *(train)*. How did it feel to read that word? I bet it felt great to master that word after all the practice you have done.	I see the hard work you are putting into your reading. Would you like to share some of the words you tackled today with the class?

Think about your own literacy instruction. What are places where you can naturally support students to grow in their happiness as readers and writers? Where can you shift your language practices to help students recognize small moments of joy in their growth as literacy learners, the value of practice, and the feelings associated with mastery? And where can you authentically recognize students and build a culture of recognition?

I often took a class list and wrote *Recognition* at the top. Every time I recognized a student for something positive, I put a check mark by their name. When you start to collect this recognition data, you might start to see that certain students routinely get recognized more than others. What if every child heard their name associated with something positive that came from hard work and strategic practice every day? The chapters to come go beyond these four simple steps, but this is a way to start right now changing your language practices to make happiness formation a core tenet of your teaching.

DESIGN FOR IT!

Before I was a teacher, I studied architecture. I learned pretty quickly that I was not very good at drawing but I was good at designing. And every design starts with a problem. As a nation, the research is clear—our children's lack of happiness is a problem. When faced with the problem of helping our students become productive and happy people, design thinking can help. Designers imagine things that don't yet exist, and then they build them, and then the world changes. But designing for happiness cannot come from spreadsheets. It has to come from kidwatching, questioning, and intentional planning. This book is here to help.

When you are a designer, you are willing to ask hard questions, and when you are willing to ask those questions, you realize you have the power to design solutions. Here are some hard questions worthy of asking that the chapters to come will help you answer:

- In what ways is connection a driving force in your literacy instruction? Does every student feel connected when they walk in the room? How can connections be strengthened?
- What are the choices you offer students as readers and writers? If more choice is given, what kind of effect would it have on students? What do you need to try to expand the choices they have?
- How do your students typically respond to challenges? How can students be supported to reframe challenges as learners as opportunities?
- How could your language choices shift to help students take ownership of their learning and have a positive narrative about themselves as learners?
- What changes would you hope to instill in your students now and for their future selves, so that they might live lives where happiness matters as much as achievement?

This book is organized to help you answer these questions and to design your literacy classroom as a place where student happiness is as great a priority as their knowledge, skills, and understanding.

Every teacher in this book is a designer. Like other kinds of designers, they don't *think* their way forward. They *build* their way forward. In education, we have frameworks for how to approach problems. One way we do that is through *if . . . then* thinking. If we do *a*, *b*, and *c . . .* then, we will get *x*, *y*, and *z*. If we use small-group instruction, then more children will get targeted attention. If we explicitly teach phonics, then more children will gain automaticity as readers. If we model with our own writing, then more children will see themselves as writers. I believe in all of these important *if . . . then* statements that are worthy of our time, attention, and consideration, and many great books have been written to help us get better at these things. This book represents the biggest *if . . . then* facing us today. If we want our children to grow up with the roots for lifelong happiness, then our schools must change. Our classrooms must change. Our instruction must change. Our relationships must change. Every chapter has this big idea in mind. Every chapter offers a pillar to stand on to know that you are designing joyful instruction with your students' happiness *and* their success as literacy learners in mind.

The seven pillars together can help you design a joyful, purposeful year that you and your students remember as a source of happiness. The first pillar, *Connection*, is designed to help you set the stage for a year of rich social and emotional connections for your students as a central part of literacy learning. If connection is why we are here, then it's the very foundation of our happiness and our classrooms. The second pillar, *Choice*, is designed to offer more specifics about the kinds of choices we can offer students as a part of literacy instruction to let students grow as readers, writers, speakers, listeners, and creators. The third pillar, *Challenge*, is designed to help you motivate students in simple, sustainable ways, so that students consistently tap into their internal motivation to outgrow themselves as literacy learners. The fourth pillar, *Play*, is designed to help you envision the ways literacy learning can be inherently playful across the grade levels. The fifth pillar, *Story*, is designed to help you make stories the heart of literacy learning so that students continuously ask "What's the story here?" whether they are reading print, digital, or multimedia texts or whether they are reading the interactions they have with others. This chapter will also help your students tell stories from their own lives and from their imaginations, giving them essential skills for making their ideas heard in the world. When we feel heard, we feel recognized. The sixth pillar, *Discovery*, is designed to help you bring a sense of awe and wonder into the literacy learning process. The final pillar, *Movement*, is designed to help you leverage the heart-mind-body connections in your students. Movement is a right for students, not a privilege.

If you want a classroom that prioritizes student happiness as much as their achievement, then this book is for you. At its heart, this book is an invitation to try something new. Hopefully, you have found inspiration in these pages already to try something new. There are many more ideas and invitations to come.

Part 1

HAPPINESS PILLARS

Chapter 2
Connection

CLASSROOM STORY: READING WITH OWEN

As I walked into Caitlin's second-grade classroom, I noticed students sitting on cushy bean-bags and in other nooks around the room. Some students were reading alone, and others were reading with partners. Some students were devouring series books while others dug into literary nonfiction and collections of poetry. Choice is a pillar that drives Caitlin's reading workshop and her students are positioned to be self-driven in their decision making. There is a calm and productive hum to the room that feels magical—this is what a reading culture is all about.

Owen is off in the corner reading the first book in the Redwall series by Brian Jacques a mighty book in a young reader's hands. When Caitlin calls everyone back to the rug for the wrap-up to reading workshop, Owen stays where he is. He doesn't leave his reading spot, and he keeps his eyes on the story in front of him. Caitlin decides to proceed without calling attention to him. The rest of the class knows that this is okay. Later, Caitlin shares with me that it is really hard to assess Owen's reading skills because whenever she confers with him he refuses to answer her questions about books. She's tried asking open-ended questions professionals suggest like "How's it going?" or inviting statements like "Tell me about what you're reading today." She has also tried asking him opinion-based questions like "What's your favorite character so far?" No matter what Caitlin has asked, she's been met with mostly silence and a slightly agitated stare. When we looked at Owen's reader response notebook, the same pattern emerged. We saw limited written responses composed mostly of simple, factual sentences about what he was reading. He wrote about his reading because he had to, not because he wanted to. When the purpose for writing about reading was preestablished by his teacher, Owen complied, albeit minimally.

Yet, to witness Owen reading is to see a young boy lost in a text the way that great stories are supposed to grab you. Everything about his physical positioning pointed to a boy who led a rich and varied reading life. When I looked out the window during recess, Owen was sitting on a bench fifty pages further into Redwall. With such a rich reading life, was it important that Owen also learn to share his thinking? Kind of. Was there a question Caitlin could ask that she hadn't tried yet that would unlock Owen's response? Probably not.

Caitlin's second grade was already a classroom where choice mattered. Students chose what they read. Where they read. Who they read with. And in Owen's case—when he read. Together, we wondered if we could take a step back to try to understand *why* Owen read. Rather than framing his reading and lack of response as a problem, we decided to look at his reading life from the lens of happiness. We started to wonder what else we could do to make Owen's thinking visible so that he could engage with someone else about his ideas as an authentic way to deepen his happiness. We needed to redesign and reframe the purpose of conferences with Owen and tie it to what research shows us about happiness. In particular, we considered the ways that we all want to feel love and belonging as a core component of being happy. While Owen was clearly a reader, he was also often alone.

Rather than ask Owen questions to elicit his response, Caitlin decided that the best way to make a reader feel like they belong is to read what the reader is reading. The other second graders were not going to be drawn to the books that Owen was reading yet, so Caitlin started reading whatever Owen was reading. Instead of asking questions that made Owen resist response, Caitlin shared her opinion about wherever she was in the book with statements like, "I'm getting worried about Matthias and the other mice. I wonder if everything is as peaceful as it seems." She didn't demand that Owen immediately respond. She backed away from peppering him with questions. Yet, once he realized that someone else cared about the same characters and events in stories that he did, Owen's responses started to shift. There was no magical question Caitlin could have asked to entice Owen to answer, but she could show him that she, too, was interested in the books and authors he was interested in to make him feel like he was part of a reading partnership.

RESEARCH SAYS: OUR BIGGEST POTENTIAL

Research on happiness and how we reach our biggest potential shows that when we focus our lives on making others happier, we in turn become happier. Not surprisingly, research also shows that people feel better on days when they have social interactions. Researcher Patricia Kuhl (2007) calls our social brain the gateway to human cognition. Even the simplest decisions like having students sit in a circle or in a *U* shape helps students tap into our primal need for connection. Think back to the happiest, most memorable moments of your life. Weddings, parties, births. For most people, these moments have one thing in common—the presence of friends or loved ones.

Balloons in the hallway

Yet, a lot of classroom instruction is focused on the concept of independent practice. But what if there was less "me" time and more "we" time? Research across fields has shown that happy people have one thing in common and it has nothing to do with their IQ, gender, or socioeconomic status: they have plenty of good relationships. This can even include interactions that psychologists call social snacking or little ways of connecting with others. For example, when people engage with fellow passengers on the train on their way to work—  whether they are introverts or extroverts—they report having a pleasant commute. Camaraderie is comforting. As adults we all know that when we talk with people on a regular basis, especially people we don't know as well, our world opens up. A true sense of belonging comes from being in relationships where you are valued for who you are and where you value others. This happens when we create spaces for students to share their stories and their thinking with their classmates as a routine, especially across many different partnerships. Literacy instruction is primed for giving students opportunities to build relationships and to feel valued.

The CEO of the Happiness Research Institute in Copenhagen, Meik Wiking, spends his days studying happiness. He leads an independent think tank focused on well-being, happiness, and quality of life. Specifically, the Happiness Research Institute studies the causes and effects of human happiness, and they work toward improving the lives of people across the world. According to their research from the European Social Survey, Danes are the happiest people in Europe. They are also the people who meet most often with their friends and family and feel the calmest. Wiking (2017) and his team have found that "the best predictor of whether we are happy (or not) is our social relationships. It is the clearest and most recurrent pattern I see when I look at the evidence on why some people are happier than others." What does that mean for our classrooms and, specifically, for literacy learning? How do we shape our classrooms to allow social relationships to flourish? How can we invite a feeling of relaxed thoughtfulness and joy into literacy learning? This chapter is my attempt to answer these questions based on years as a classroom teacher, literacy specialist, literacy coach, and teacher educator.

I like to think that teachers are really memory makers. Every lesson at its core is designed with the intention of helping young people build lasting memories so that they can retrieve what they've learned and apply it in a new way. If we want students to remember the things

Anchor Chart to Support
Student Emotions

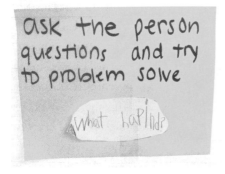

Anchor Chart to Support
Student Emotions

they experience in school, then joy has to be the overriding feeling they experience. The best way I know to ensure that literacy learning is joyful and memorable is to foster deep and meaningful connections between you and your students and between your students and each other.

Studies consistently show that our own happiness is linked with the happiness of those around us. The Framingham Heart Study is a massive study that started in 1948 tracking three generations of participants. To measure happiness, the researchers asked participants how often they experienced certain feelings during the previous week:

- I felt hopeful about the future.
- I was happy.
- I enjoyed life.
- I felt that I was just as good as other people.

Harvard scientists then mined the data to study happiness and social networks (Fowler and Christakis 2008). They concluded that people's happiness depends on the happiness of others with whom they are connected. People who are surrounded by many happy people are more likely to become happy in the future. Each additional happy friend increases your chance of happiness by about 9 percent. All of this points to the deep need for connection to be the first pillar of happiness in our classrooms.

As teachers, we can intentionally strengthen the connections between students as a part of literacy learning. Pam Allyn and Ernest Morrell (2016) remind us in their book *Every Child a Super Reader: 7 Strengths to Open a World of Possible* that feelings of connection and belonging have everything to do with literacy. They write, "First, belonging to a community and feeling safe, positive, and happy in it helps children become empowered and more connected to the work that is required within the class." They add, "Secondly, when the community identifies itself by its very nature as a group of avid readers and hard-working authors, the children's identity becomes tied to that definition" (43).

We know that making connections is at the heart of learning and creativity. Even the youngest children make connections as a way to make sense of the world. Early literacy is built on the power of connections as children learn that sounds stand for words and that words stand for people, places, or things they know. There are countless ways books, stories, and storytelling strengthen our connections not only to texts but to one another.

In this chapter, I share structures and instructional strategies you can use to support students to deepen connections to one another as part of reading, writing, and communicating. Throughout the chapter, I also recommend children's books that gave me and my students a deep sense of connection. Books I connect to and want to share with students may not be the same as yours, but these examples are intentionally shared as books that invite the possibility for your students to connect with each other in new and powerful ways.

READ-ALOUD AS THE DAILY SPARK

In John's fourth grade, as in many classrooms, the read-aloud is a sacred time each day. His students gather on the rug propped on pillows, and they find spots along the window seat. His voice takes them to emotional places. One of John's favorite books is *Because of Mr. Terupt* (Buyea 2011), which features seven narrators, each with a unique story, and each with a different perspective on what makes their teacher so special. John's students are encouraged to tap into their own emotions as he is reading and to notice what makes them feel something strongly. When they transition to independent reading, they look for places in their books where they have a strong feeling, and they are encouraged to linger there—to pause and mentally take note of their reactions and to connect those feelings to their own lives. When his students return to the rug during the wrap-up time, they are asked what about their reading today made them better people, not just better readers. Essentially, he asks them, "How are you changed?"

In John's classroom, the read-aloud is a nonnegotiable daily structure. It is the daily spark to support students to not only grow as readers of words but to grow as readers of the world (Friere and Macedo 1987). He reads aloud novels that take several weeks to finish. He also reads a variety of picture books where the illustrations are integral to the understanding of the story. His students sit on the edge of their seats eager to hear the characters' latest challenges, triumphs, and tribulations. He also reads books that inspire students to consider who they will be in the world and to consider how they will help others. While he often reads books that evoke laughter, not every book selection he makes is humorous. But, every book he reads is designed to spark deep thought, connection, and the comfort of hearing a story well-told—it's a joyful ritual each day.

John reads aloud books like *The Three Questions* by Jon Muth (2002), recast from a Tolstoy short story into a picture book format. In Muth's version, a boy named Nikolai believes that if he can find the answer to his three questions then he will know how to be a good person. Nikolai feels uncertain just like we all do. As readers, we are left satisfied by the end, but inevitably we are left with more questions than answers. John knows this, and his reading of the book inspires his students to question what they think they know about how to be a good person and how to live a good life. The conversation that ensues afterward is complex, worthwhile, and philosophical in nature. John recognizes that the thinking that takes place during and after the read-aloud is some of the most formative thinking his students engage in each day.

The time we spend reading aloud is like no other time. There is no substitute for the read-aloud. As teachers, we are the strongest readers in the room, and our voices can carry students to far-off places and the innermost corners of their minds. The *Kids and Family Reading Report: The Rise of the Read-Aloud* (Scholastic 2019) found that parents reading aloud to children at home is on the rise, up nearly 50 percent from 2014 with 43 percent of parents reporting that their children were read to essentially since birth. The report also found that 83 percent of children who are or have been read to loved or liked it a lot and that 85 percent of children say it is a special time with their family. Although read-aloud frequency is also on the rise, it diminishes rapidly as children grow older, peaking at five years old with dramatic declines with each additional year of age. Scholastic data also show a disparity among lower- and higher-income households with children ages eight and under read to less frequently, ranging from 39 percent among families with household incomes less than $35,000 compared with 62 percent among families with incomes of $100,000 or more. Limited access to books in lower-income communities helps explain these data. Although promising, these data also show us that the read-aloud at school is critical for students when we know there are disparities and drop-offs of read-aloud routines at home once children reach school age. When the read-aloud is a daily expectation at school, we nurture all students to make personal connections that inspire them to think and feel more deeply and wholeheartedly.

Reading aloud is the very foundation of literacy learning. As explained by several leading literacy researchers, it is the single most important activity for reading success (Neuman, Copple, and Bredekamp 2000). It supports vocabulary acquisition, syntactic knowledge, comprehension, fluency, and student writing. It reveals the rewards of reading and develops the listener's interest in books and desire to be a reader (Mooney 1990). It broadens students' thinking as well as their imaginations (Coiro 2000) and supports emotional intelligence (Sullivan and Strang 2002). When we hear a story well told, we connect to the characters, their situations, or the settings where the story takes place. We also recognize that we have the same fears, interests, and concerns as characters. Perhaps most importantly, a read-aloud routine helps students start to tell their own stories, which builds connections between students. Steven Layne (2015) describes in his book *In Defense of Read-Aloud: Sustaining Best Practice* that he would hang a Do Not Disturb sign on his door to demonstrate the class commitment to the daily read-aloud.

In addition to all the literacy learning benefits, brain and behavioral science also show us that reading aloud is more than just a simple, classroom pastime of one person reading to others. It is fuel for the heart, mind, and imagination. Brain scans, particularly from The Cincinnati Children's Reading and Literacy Discovery Center, now show us that reading aloud picture books, in particular, stimulates children's deep brain networks, fostering optimal cognitive development while also cultivating language acquisition and empathy. The read-aloud invites neural networks to fire and connect with one another. As Meghan Cox Gurdon (2019) explains in *The Enchanted Horse: The Miraculous Power of Reading Aloud in the Age of Distraction*, "The evidence has become so overwhelming that social scientists now consider read-aloud time one of the most important indicators of a children's prospects in life" (xiv). As compared with touch screens that scatter our brains and our attention, a story read aloud fosters deep, sustained attention. If reading aloud is a source of emotional and intellectual nourishment, imagine how the world would look if every child had stories read aloud to them every day at school.

The benefits to reading aloud are also cumulative across our lifetimes. The traces of stories and voices become a part of us as embedded memories that shape what we think, how we feel, and how we act. Gurdon states it this way: "The story of humankind is the story of the human voice, telling stories" (20). A daily commitment to the read-aloud is not only a daily commitment to modeling confident and fluent reading, but also a daily commitment to students' lifelong, sustainable happiness.

EMPATHY BUILDING THROUGH LITERATURE

Over time, daily read-alouds create a sense of love and belonging in our students. The literature we choose to read aloud and the books that line our classroom bookshelves have the power to change our students as literacy learners and also, more importantly, as people. Helping our students to become empathetic may be one of the most challenging, but important, roles we play. While our own modeling of empathy that we extend toward our students and our colleagues creates a ripple effect, drawing from characters as models turns those ripples into waves. Some of our students will struggle with empathy. At times, we all do. When we encourage students to read with a lens toward "I never knew" and "Me, too" moments, they will begin to apply that thinking to their own lives and relationships with others. Brené Brown's work on vulnerability, shame, and worthiness points to the human need we all have to feel love and belonging as a core tenet of building a life of happiness. One concept she returns to particularly in her book, *Braving the Wilderness: The Quest for True Belonging and the Courage to Stand Alone* (2017), is the importance of cultivating empathy. She explains that empathy has four qualities: the ability to take the perspective of another person, staying away from judgment, recognizing emotion in others, and communicating it. She defines empathy as "feeling with people." One of the most powerful ways we have of supporting students to understand these qualities of empathy and in turn to become more empathetic is through literature.

Any literature that grapples with big ideas and stirs up strong emotions offers a site for building empathy. Yet, some books position us to think, act, and feel in more empathetic ways. When I curate collections of books to build a more empathetic world, I look for any story that helps readers recognize that everyone loves someone and everyone struggles with something. The following are some ways of thinking about the purposes of literature whether you are selecting a book for a read-aloud to build empathy or you are looking for titles for book clubs or independent reading. These stories evoke a range of emotions and show students that the cultivation of happiness comes from accepting all of the emotions you feel.

Stories with Characters We Care About

There are some characters that we root for from the beginning of a book because they have experienced hardship and we want it to all work out in the end. Or because they need something and we want to see them reach their goal. Or because they take a stand even when it's hard to do so.

Writing for an early childhood audience, Mo Willems has the extraordinary ability of making us care about Elephant and Piggie, book after book. We empathize with Piggie and Gerald in *My Friend Is Sad* (Willems 2007) because we have all experienced sadness and we have witnessed the sadness of others. Willems follows in the tradition of the Frog and Toad series by Arnold Lobel (1970). We care whether Frog and Toad can overcome their fears in "Dragons and Giants," and we empathize when they eat cookie after cookie and eventually give away their baked goods to the birds because it's easier than having willpower in "Cookies."

Stories with compelling, likable characters have always been intertwined with feelings of empathy like Miss Honey in *Matilda* by Roald Dahl (1988), Lucy Pevensie in *The Lion, the Witch, and the Wardrobe* (Lewis 1950), and Charlie and Grandpa Joe in *Charlie and the Chocolate Factory* (Dahl 1964). These are characters any reader would be hard-pressed to find something negative to say about them because they actively strive to make the lives of others better. They are selfless. They are striving for a better world through their words and actions. They inspire feelings of altruism in us as readers.

Contemporary picture books foster feelings of empathy through the words and the illustrations. *Those Shoes* by Maribeth Boelts (2009) tells the story of Jeremy, who yearns for a pair of black high tops with three white stripes. He saves up his own money and buys a pair too small for his feet at the thrift store. He wears them uncomfortably, and our toes ache alongside Jeremy's. But, he shows us he cares more about others when he anonymously delivers the shoes to the doorstep of a boy who needs them more than he does. Books like *We're All Wonders* by R. J. Palacio (2017), based on the best-selling novel, *Wonder* (Palacio 2012), and *One* by Katherine Otoshi (2008) inspire readers to realize that we are all worthy of one another's respect and that we have more in common than we have differences.

Stories with Characters We Don't Immediately Root For

Must heroes of children's literature always be likeable? Think about Severus Snape in Harry Potter. We think early on in the series that Severus is a hard-nosed professor who dislikes Harry, Ron, and Hermione simply out of spite. Yet, by book two we realize that Severus has a history and a backstory where bullying from classmates left him vulnerable and alone. Our perception of Severus starts to slowly shift the more we learn about his motives and his child-hood story. We don't immediately root for Professor Snape, but over the series our feelings start to change. When this happens, we realize that if we are capable of changing our minds about characters, maybe we are capable of changing our minds about people in our lives, too. This is how empathy grows.

Or think about Gru from *Despicable Me*. Gru is a villain. He wants to destroy the world with his rocket. But three girls enter his life, and he shows us he is capable of great change. When we see flashbacks to his childhood, we realize his mother never recognized his inter-ests or affirmed him through positive praise. We realize none of the kids on the playground wanted "gruties," a particularly hurtful term for "cooties." Watching these scenes, we change our minds about Gru, and his changes as a character help inspire changes in ourselves.

Or think about the Grinch in Dr. Seuss' classic holiday tale *How the Grinch Stole Christ-mas* (1957). It has been rereleased as a film both in animation and through live action several times over the decades and yet the message remains the same. "Well, in Whoville they say— that the Grinch's small heart grew three sizes that day." When we witness this change, we start to think, if the Grinch's heart can grow, so can mine. So can anyone's. Empathy is not about having a character that is innately likable. Empathy is inspired when we read literature or view or hear stories where a character helps us say "me, too." I am flawed. I am capable of change. I am worthy of love and belonging.

We also have characters like Greg Heffley in *Diary of a Wimpy Kid* (Kinney 2007) whose diary is a commentary on what everyone else is like. The appeal of the character for generations of boys, in particular, has been his "every boy" quality. And we have characters like Pigeon in Mo Willems' (2003) *Don't Let the Pigeon Drive the Bus!* Pigeon is rascally. He disregards boundaries. He'll do just about anything to get his way. But, by the end, we find ourselves rooting for him.

When students encounter characters that they don't immediately root for, we can support them to consider where good lives in the characters or to look closely at the charac-ter's actions, words, and feelings to understand what their motives are and how they might change if they were shown kindness by others.

Stories About People from Other Places

When we first encounter books with characters that are from other parts of the world, or from other neighborhoods, we may leap to judgment, particularly if we have little practice assuming connection instead of disconnection. Reading global literature helps students realize that their story is not the only story, but it also helps them recognize the ways people everywhere have the same hopes and dreams. Picture books like *Marwan's Journey* by Patricia de Arias (2018) help young readers realize the journey, uncertainty, and eventual hope of a refugee child. Middle-grade novels like Katherine Applegate's *Wishtree* (2017) help us realize the stigma and hardship recent immigrants may experience. Yet, we are left as readers with far more hope than despair for the possibility of good neighbors, of communities rising together, and we are given a road map for how to foster a sense of belonging. Books like *The Breadwinner* by Deborah Ellis (2000), now an animated film, help middle-grade readers to understand the constraints and risks of children of war. In all of these stories and in many works of global literature, children are the heroes. We can intentionally design for students to become more empathetic when we make our literature selections purposeful and meaningful and when we design our read-alouds to ensure we expose students to global stories with compelling characters.

Stories That Represent Diverse Society

Selecting a wide range of diverse books helps all children find and make connections to their own life experiences, other books they have read, and universal concepts (Dyson and Genishi 1994). When the books we read aloud represent diverse society, we help all children see themselves in books, but we also give them what Christopher Myers (2014) calls a "literary roadmap" for shaping their lives. Thanks to the efforts of authors, illustrators, scholars, and publishers of color, the landscape of children's literature is becoming more diverse. Books that represent diverse society are no longer relegated to civil rights stories or biographies of people from the past. Today some of the most important works of children's literature include everyday stories and imaginative tales where the characters represent the full human experience. Books like Newbery-winning *Last Stop on Market Street* by Matt de la Peña (2015), *Tiny, Perfect Things* by M.H. Clark (2018), *The Word Collector* by Peter Reynolds (2018), *Over and Under the Pond* by Kate Messner (2017), and *Ocean Meets Sky* by Terry and Eric Fan (2018) all include diverse characters where the characters' race or ethnicity is not central to the storyline. Rather, the characters' diversity adds depth and authenticity to the stories.

Think about the characters your students explore through your read-alouds and that line your classroom bookshelf. How do they inspire empathy? In what ways can you make connections explicit for students by helping them to consider how characters overcome odds, how characters change over the course of a story, and how characters can build a more just world? The following are some guiding questions adapted from Gold and Gibson's (2001) guide on reading aloud to build comprehension to help you select books for read-alouds to build a sense of empathy in students:

- Is it a good story?
- Will my students connect to the characters?
- Do the characters model empathy?
- Do the characters model change in some way?
- Will my students find the book relevant to their lives?
- Will the book spark conversation?
- Will the book motivate deeper understanding of people and/or other parts of the world?
- Does the book inspire children to find or listen to another book on the same topic? By the same author? Written in the same genre?
- Is the story memorable?
- Will children want to hear the story again?

PERSPECTIVE-TAKING OR "PEOPLE SENSE"

Have you ever known someone in your life who really listens when you speak? Doesn't it feel good to know you are being heard and that your ideas are valued even if the person doesn't agree? These tend to be people in your life with a lot of "people sense." They tend to feel comfortable looking you in the eye. They ask follow-up questions when you speak like

"So, what did you do next?" or "What else do you think?" They know how to say things like "Tell me more" and to respond to what you've said. The older I get, the more conscious I find myself of building circles of friends that are really good at listening, who are willing to share their own stories, and who value my perspective. Perspective-taking is the ability to see points of view other than your own. Perspective-taking is more than having empathy, as critical as that is. Perspective-taking is really understanding the goals and intentions of others. It's a true social-emotional-intellectual life skill. Sometimes it can feel like some people are just better at perspective-taking than others, but the truth is we can all get better at this with a little purposeful practice and by having some strategies for how to get better at it. Children feel these dynamics, too. They are sometimes quick to think that some children in class are just better at having people sense. But when we design instruction to strengthen all of our students' people sense, our students grow in confidence by design, not by chance.

According to Galinsky's (2010) research on child brain development explained in *Mind in the Making*, perspective-taking involves *inhibitory control* (inhibit our own thoughts and feelings to be open to others), *cognitive flexibility* (to see a situation in different ways), and *reflection* (consider the thoughts of others as well as our own). We see this in children in our classrooms that know what teachers and their peers want and expect. But there is an important connection between what's going on in the brain for people who have people sense and reading. To understand how reading and language works is to understand something about what others are thinking. To anticipate it in a way. Not only do students become stronger readers when perspective-taking is nurtured, but they also become more compassionate, capable, and adaptable when perspective-taking becomes a strength.

One of the great gifts literature gives us is the chance to imagine life from the perspective of someone else. When we read stories where the characters feel real, we hear their internal thoughts and we experience some of their pain. As readers, when we experience that connectedness to characters again and again, we start to realize that our perspective may not be the only perspective. We need perspective-taking for social interaction, academic success, and personal problem solving. We need perspective-taking to form meaningful and lasting friendships, to listen to others and respond, and, ultimately, to build sustained happiness. Understanding what other people in our life think and feel is heightened by having a strong narrative comprehension. Analyzing characters' thoughts, feelings, intentions, actions, and plans helps students to better understand the perspectives different characters have. Some books also position readers to understand multiple perspectives about a given event. *They All Saw a Cat* by Brendan Wenzel (2016) is a fun book for any age to reinforce the idea that even when you are at the same place looking at the same thing as someone else, your versions might be different. *Red: A Crayon's Story* by Michael Hall (2015) eases students into the idea that who we think we are isn't always the same as how others perceive us. It's a gentle introduction to complex identity concepts, especially when we give students the space to direct the conversation about the reactions to the story through open-ended questions.

Fairy-tale units have also been full of examples of playing with perspective-taking particularly when traditional tales are read alongside fractured fairy tales like *The Three Little Wolves and the Big Bad Pig* (Trivizas 1997), *Little Red Writing* (Holub 2016), and my favorite, *The Paperbag Princess* (Munsch 1980). Crayons, animals, and imaginative twists on traditional characters are joyful, lighthearted ways to open up conversations that foster perspective-taking. But human characters that seem like you or me are important for children to see themselves in stories and to realize their story is not the only story.

Why Am I Me? by Paige Britt (2017) is the fictional story of two children who notice one another on a train asking themselves, "Why am I me . . . and not you? Why are you, you . . . and not me?" These seemingly simple, yet profoundly philosophical questions are made to feel familiar for children, urging them to ask big questions about themselves and others. Books that celebrate diversity and our shared humanity are becoming more prevalent, giving students the chance to see themselves in stories while also learning about the life experiences of others. The cover illustration of *Why Am I Me?* brilliantly shows the overlap we have as human beings while also celebrating the ways no one else is you or me. Students that grow in their perspective-taking recognize that we are all people with various identities, but we all share some fundamental qualities as humans. There are many high-quality books that open up conversations about identity, community, and shared qualities of being human to support students to build intercultural understandings. Some others I love are: *Same, Same, but Different* by Jenny Sue Kostecki-Shaw (2011); *Same Sun Here* by Silas House and Neela Vaswani (2012); *Most People* by Michael Leannah (2017); *Lovely* by Jess Hong (2017); *No One Else Like You* by Siska Goeminne (2017); *The Colors of Us* by Karen Katz (2002); *Whoever You Are* by Mem Fox (1997); *Skin Again* by bell hooks (2004); *Shades of People* by Sheila M. Kelly (2009); and *Let's Talk About Race* by Julius Lester (2008). These books invite students to make meaningful text-to-self, text-to-text, text-to-world, and text-to-other conversations. In your own classroom and school library, look for texts like these to spark conversations with students about the characters as well as the connections and disconnections students have to the characters, setting, and storylines. These books and the conversations that spring from them help students grow people sense by design rather than leaving it to chance.

There are also things we can do as teachers to model perspective-taking for students:

- Repeat back students' words or what you think they were trying to say.
- Model not knowing and what you can do to find out.
- Express compassion for others publicly.
- Talk about your own feelings.

DEEPENING CONVERSATION

For perspective-taking to become something students really thrive at beyond a single unit or set time of the year, we can encourage students to share their thinking openly and often. Through deep conversation, ideas do not simply accumulate; they are explored and wrestled with (Barnes and Todd 1995; Wilkinson and Son 2011). Dialogic teaching runs counter to prescripted, tightly controlled instruction specified in many literacy curricula. In fact, dialogue and discussion have long been linked to theories of democratic education. From Socrates to Dewey and Habermas, educative dialogue has represented a forum for learners to develop understanding by listening, reflecting, proposing, and incorporating alternative views.

Yet, supporting students to be accountable in their talk ensures that conversation doesn't become "anything goes." Lauren Resnick, Sarah Michaels, and Catherine O'Connor (2008) suggest the three principals of accountable talk, and many others discuss the vision of their effectiveness in the classroom:

1. Accountability to the learning community: the talk should "attend seriously to and build on the ideas of others."

2. Accountability to standards of reasoning: the talk should "emphasize logical connections and the drawing of reasonable conclusions" on the basis of premises and argumentation.

3. Accountability to knowledge: the talk should be "based explicitly on facts, written texts or other . . . information that all . . . can access. Speakers make an effort to get their facts right and make explicit the evidence behind their claims and expectations. They challenge each other when evidence is lacking or unavailable" (283).

If we want students to become critical members of society who converse, interpret, question, and challenge the world around them, we need to support them with strategies and models of language. In *Conversations: Strategies for Teaching, Learning, and Evaluating*, Regie Routman (2000) explains, "All learning involves conversation. The ongoing dialogue, internal and external, that occurs as we read, write, listen, compose, observe, refine, interpret, and analyze is how we learn" (xxxvi). Students need opportunities to listen to their peers, consider any points made, and respond to them in a critical way.

Some language frames I've given students that really help set the tone that perspective-taking is important include:

- Yes, and _____ .
- Yes, but _____ .
- No, because _____ .
- Tell me more about _____ .
- I know what you mean by _____ .
- I don't know what you mean by _____ .
- It might be _____ .
- Maybe it actually is _____ .
- Could it be _____ ?

These phrases can support students to say more about literature and other classroom engagements, but they are also applicable on the playground, in the hallway, on the sports field, or at the dinner table. It can be hard for children to let others know that they don't know something or to ask for clarification. It can also be hard for children to let their peers know that they are on their side or that they might have a different idea. Finally, it's hard for anyone to sometimes show others you are listening, but phrases like "tell me more" work well as conversation continuers to show you care about what the other person is saying.

In Kelly's fourth-grade reading class, she wanted to move students from being "*I*-centered" in their discussions to support her students to listen with intention and to build on what others are saying. When she started leaning in to their conversations, she found that they were not listening to their partner's comments nor were they using their partner's comments to inform their thinking. Kelly knew that this was more than a classroom skill but rather a life skill. She video recorded student conversations about books, transcribed their talk, and analyzed the impact of introducing the previous sentence frames on her students' discussion. She found that given these new language frames, they were able to respond to one another's ideas, and the overuse of *I* statements became less dominant in their talk.

After reading aloud *The Raft* by Jim Lamarche (2000), Kelly's students talked about how Nicky and his grandma's relationship was changing using "yes, and" and "yes, but" to grow their discussion:

Alexis: Their relationship is changing because Nicky is doing what his grandma is doing.

Emmanuel: Yes, but their relationship is changing because when Nicky found the raft, Grandma actually got him interested in animals. So, then, when he started to see all these animals he started to get interested in them and they started talking. Eventually they started talking about how she draws animals and what she does.

After reading aloud *The Invisible Boy* by Trudy Ludwig (2013), Kelly's students had the following exchanges about a scene in the book where the boy wished he could draw a hole that would swallow him up:

Alexis: It might be because he's invisible, it says he's invisible [*pointing to the book*], so, um, that's what I think.

Emmanuel: Maybe it is actually because no one really notices him because if he's going in that order and he still doesn't get picked he basically has no friends. I would feel like that if I had no friends.

Alexis: Yeah, I would feel black and white. It might also be that, um, he's probably feeling sad. If someone doesn't notice me or want to be my friend, I would feel sad.

This kind of discussion does not emerge by accident but rather by design. When Kelly looked back at all of the transcripts she had from her students' read-aloud conversations, she concluded that the talk strategies lifted the level of student thinking and oral language when (1) the talk stems were open ended; (2) the talk stems used language such as *might, could,* and *maybe*, so as to help students explore multiple possibilities; and (3) time was devoted to practice the newly implemented strategies. Kelly had moved her students from trying to "outsmart" one another to having sophisticated, meaningful conversations about books where they considered their own and others' points of view.

FROM PARTNERSHIPS TO CLUBS

Social connection brings us joy and can start small through simple partnerships that help students say more and help them clarify what they think and feel. Once students have a strong partnership routine established where they are comfortable turning and talking to a partner during a read-aloud, consider forming partnerships in other ways throughout the day. One way to extend students' time with texts is to balance independent reading with partner reading. There are many variations on partner reading, but some include choral reading, where students read the same text aloud at the same time; partner reading, where students alternate sentences, paragraphs, or pages; and echo reading, where one partner reads and then another partner reads the same text. We see these partnerships more frequently in the lower elementary grades as students grow in their fluency and accuracy with more and more exposure to print. When these partnerships are a daily expectation, students come to look forward to their partner time as a way to socially connect through their reading. As students get older, it's essential to maintain that social connection through reading, if possible on a daily basis. Even reserving the last five minutes of independent reading for partner reading time in upper elementary and middle school grades allows for literacy learning to be positioned as a social practice, not just an independent one. Upper elementary school students benefit from connection as much as anyone, and sometimes that connection can come from reading partners that talk about what they are reading, but they can also use partnerships as a time to read something together through choral, partner, or echo reading.

Other kinds of partnerships include conversation partners that share their reactions to texts at the end of independent reading or before beginning (to share their reading plans for the day). Not only do partners grow in their thinking about their own books through conversation, but they are also able to serve as each other's book mentors by hearing about the reading adventures their partners are having with a variety of texts. When reading partnerships include conversations about books where one participant may not know the text yet, it sparks a reading culture that is contagious.

Writing partnerships matter just as much as reading partnerships. When peers gain comfort with others looking at and giving feedback on their writing, you know you have a strong writing culture in your classroom. There are many ways teachers facilitate writing partner talk so that students don't find themselves mentally engaged in "compare-despair." That is, sometimes the process of looking at someone else's writing can make you feel like an imposter or less skilled than someone else. Because the act of writing is such a vulnerable process, it's important to carefully consider writing partnerships so that students benefit from the social connection as writers, not so that they are correcting, comparing, or despairing over their writing. One way to make writing partnerships more about social connection is to initially limit partnerships to only offer compliments. As students are comfortable giving specific compliments about what they like in each other's writing and artwork, introduce the idea of a compliment sandwich where students can be invited to share a compliment-question-compliment. Learning how to ask the right question is a lifelong skill and is at the heart of effective communication. The least judgmental kinds of questions are usually questions that further the thinking of the writer (rather than questions that are really masked suggestions à la "What if you tried . . ."). Rather students can be supported to ask questions like:

- What are you working on?
- How can I help?
- What do you like most in your piece?
- What is something you are thinking of changing?
- How did you decide on _____ ?

As students gain comfort with partnerships, two partnerships can become a club. This broadens the social connection dynamic and works especially well when partnerships have had a few weeks to flourish. Clubs that have two partnerships that have already been working well together are sometimes more effective at giving everyone a voice than clubs composed of members that have never met together before. The club dynamic to avoid is one or two students taking the lead with everyone else taking a back seat to the conversation. One protocol to establish to help clubs flourish is to instill a "three before me" mindset. Some classrooms use this phrasing to encourage students to ask each other for help. This phrasing also works well so that students make sure three people have given ideas before they give a second idea. This requires that some students speak up and others give up air space that they desperately want to fill. This protocol also helps adults interact with one another more civilly, respectfully, and mindfully and ensures the inclusion of everyone's ideas.

The more we can honor the social lives and needs of our students while they are in our care, the more we can help them realize that their perspective is valued but it is also not the only perspective. We can help them find belonging by reading stories that model inclusion and a just society. We can create routines that help them find their voice and help them learn to listen. We can intentionally design our instruction with consideration of the value

[handwritten marginal note: Square your pair]

of play at every age and every stage. When we make literacy learning a social practice, we not only strengthen students' literacy skills but we communicate that happiness is as much of a priority as success.

DAILY GRATITUDE AND AFFIRMATION

One of the simplest ways to foster connection and start with joy is to nurture a sense of daily gratitude and affirmation. In Chapter 1, I introduced five-minute journaling and explained the results I found with Veronica and Monique, two fourth-grade teachers. This is a daily journaling practice that helps students practice gratitude and affirm their worth and their sense of self every day. But there are other ways of supporting especially younger children to practice daily gratitude and self-affirmation particularly through classroom routines rooted in connection.

In Alison's kindergarten class, each day the children go around the closing circle at the end of the day holding a stuffed ladybug sharing something they are proud of from their day or something about how they felt. Alison is a kindergarten teacher who knows that children need opportunities to internalize their pride every day as a way to design for happiness. She knows that there will not always be a teacher or adult nearby to offer children constant praise, nor would that benefit them. Instead, she tries to instill in them the joy that can come from self-acknowledgment. She supports her young learners to be able to tell themselves "I did a good job" and to know they are speaking the truth. The daily closing circle routine gives her students a chance to share their experiences from the day with others, shifting the learning from something that feels self-driven to something that is social. The end results are intense feelings of worthiness that come from a sense of belonging when you know that others have listened to your daily thoughts and affirmations of yourself. Alison does not leave this to chance but rather commits to the closing circle routine every day for students to reflect, share, and listen to others. The time commitment is only about five minutes, much like five-minute journaling, but the long-term benefits for the children in her care to learn about themselves and others provide a foundation for sustainable happiness.

In addition to the closing routine each day, in Alison's kindergarten children are encouraged simply to be nicer. Each student is given a special kindness token at the start of the year that they can pass on to others in the class or at home when they catch someone in the act of doing something kind. The tokens are small, ceramic tiles that the children choose. When they pass theirs on to someone else, they know they may get it back in return, but they may get someone else's. Her students were also encouraged at the start of each week to try to do three to five acts of kindness a week. Her suggestions are simple. Let someone ahead of you in line. Give another student or someone at home a compliment. Smile at someone you don't know.

Alison knows that connection, especially social connection, sets a classroom community in motion. This kind of connection creates an unshakable foundation for which students can build a lifetime of joyful learning. Yet, growing a sense of gratitude and self-affirmation doesn't come from experiences we engage in once in a while. For gratitude and self-affirmation to stick, for it to become a part of us, it has to be a ritual that can be looked forward to. In fact, research summarized in *Scientific American* (Kaufman 2015) found that gratitude is the single best predictor for well-being and good relationships, beating out twenty-four other impressive traits such as hope, love, and creativity. Alison's classroom has many different kinds of opportunities to practice daily gratitude and self-affirmation with a particular emphasis on fostering connections among her students. She does not leave these mindsets to chance. Instead, she is intentional in designing the classroom experiences to ensure that these practices are a daily commitment for her and her students' well-being.

MAY THE FORCE OF OTHERS BE WITH YOU

One of the incredible things about life is that for all the years we spend in schools, success is defined by individual attributes. But then in adulthood, most of our successes are entirely interconnected to others. When I talk to people about happiness, one of the first things I usually hear is how happiness is a choice. We choose to be happy. While I believe that's true, happiness is not just an individual choice; it is an interconnected one.

In his groundbreaking book on human happiness, *Big Potential*, Shawn Achor (2018) explains how the famed line from Star Wars "May the Force be with you" was not in the original script. What was originally written was "May the Force of *others* be with you." Research at Harvard Medical School has found that if you become happier, any friend in a one-mile radius would be 63 percent more likely to be happy. Wow. What does that mean if our classrooms can boost children's happiness by design? Research on how to reach our big potential in life shows that happiness does not come from success; rather, it's the reverse—that when we are more happy, we are more successful. But the true key to finding happiness is finding joy in helping others become happier. Happiness really is a renewable resource that we can design instruction around to help students reach their biggest potential. Strengthening connection is the first pillar for how to get there.

DESIGN FOR CONNECTION

- Happiness list making
- Beginning-of-the-year prompts:

    What three words best describe you?

    What is unique about you that leads to your happiest times?

    What are your strengths, and how can you use them?

- Five-minute journaling routine:

    I am grateful for _____ .

What would make today great?

I am _____ .

_____ was amazing today.

Something I learned today _____ .

- Read aloud every day
- Sharing stories:

    With characters we care about

    With characters we don't immediately root for

    About people from other places

    That represent diverse society

- Reading closure questions:

    What made you a better reader today?

    What made you a better person?

    How did characters help you figure that out?

- Deepening conversation through sentence frames:

    Yes, and _____ .

    Yes, but _____ .

    No, because _____ .

    Tell me more about _____ .

    I know what you mean by _____ .

    I don't know what you mean by _____ .

- Partnerships and club prompts:

  What are you working on?

  How can I help?

  What do you like most in your piece?

  What is something you are thinking of changing?

  How did you decide on _____ ?

- Daily gratitude and affirmation:

  Closure question each day: What did you do today that made someone else happy?

  Gratitude class lists

  Gratitude class jar

Chapter 3

Choice

I am seeking, I am striving,
I am in it with all my heart.

—Vincent Van Gogh

CLASSROOM STORY: A CLASSROOM LIBRARY FOR SELF-DRIVEN CHILDREN

Feeling in control of our own destiny, or having agency, is critical to finding and sustaining our own happiness. Stacy's first-grade classroom library is well organized and accessible for her students. There are bins based on topic, genre, series, and author, but you won't find bins that are leveled. Stacy's students have been empowered from Day One to know that their choices as readers are as important as learning how to read. Making a book choice is the first act a reader must do. The book choices her students make are all appropriate because their decision-making process is purposeful, authentic, and valued. The first conferences Stacy has with students each year are to talk with her students about the books they've chosen so that she can hear their logic about why this book is a match for them. Stacy trusts their choices every time.

By intentionally building a classroom library that is organized, but not leveled, Stacy has supported her students to be self-driven and agentive. Ned Johnson and William Stixrud (2018), as described in their book, *The Self-Driven Child: The Science and Sense of Giving Your Kids More Control over Their Lives*, found that giving kids more control over their lives increases their intrinsic motivation. This is fundamental to supporting children to be happier at home, but it is also critical to children's happiness in school. We must trust children to make their own choices. Rather than micromanaging their experiences, we must step back as educators and instead frame learning as a constant choice. Yes, you can choose whether you wear a jacket outside. Yes, you can choose whether you sit or stand. Yes, you can choose the kind of book you want to read. As teachers, we can make instructional decisions that facilitate student choice by design. We can begin by asking ourselves questions like: How can I help this child gain a sense of control over their (reading/writing) life?

RESEARCH SAYS: WHY CHOICE DRIVES AGENCY

Remember your own early reading life. Remember taking yourself to the furthest corner of the room with a book you just had to read. Come bedtime, remember the feeling of reading under the covers with a flashlight hoping no one would tell you to turn it off. I would bet that the books in your hands were chosen by you. Not by a teacher or a parent. By you.

If access to books and opportunities for choice help build skilled readers, what gets in the way? We know that lives in schools are complicated. There are frequent unintended interruptions like announcements and schedule changes. Classroom library collections may be minimal or outdated. The books available may not represent the readers in the room or our diverse society. And, as teachers, we also unintentionally get in the way when we pepper students with questions, turn reading into required jotting, and limit students' choices. So how can we redesign our instruction to make choice more authentic and sustainable? And why is this so important?

For decades, leading voices in the field, supported by research, have advocated for choice to drive students' reading lives. All of this research shows us that choice matters. Books matter. Belonging matters. To be a self-driven reader or writer is to feel validated in your decision making. If we want children to *want* to read and write, not just know *how* to read and write, then choice is the next pillar of happiness that schools and classrooms can design for. Ultimately, empowering children to be self-driven by giving them choices in their learning is an act of caring. When we open up our classrooms as spaces designed for authentic choice, we support children to be intrinsically motivated, which can boost student learning. We know as educators that when children are engaged and energized by their learning, they learn more and remember the experience for a longer period of time.

As explained by Mike Anderson (2016) in *Learning to Choose, Choosing to Learn: The Key to Student Motivation and Achievement*, giving students the power of choice helps overcome two distinct classroom challenges: how to differentiate learning and student apathy to learning. The reasons choice works as a motivator are abundant. One reason choice works is that it gives students control over finding their own appropriate challenge. Challenges that feel right make us want to try again and again. Another reason choice works is because it supports students to tap into their interests and passions by noticing what brings them joy. A third reason choice works as a motivator is because of the recursive power of repeated positive emotions that come from choice. Our brains crave positive emotions, including the feelings that come from making effective, self-driven choices. Feelings of boredom and stress that can come from a lack of choices sends the brain into stress-mode, which shuts down learning.

Daniel Pink (2009) wrote, "Control leads to compliance; autonomy leads to engagement" (108). When our classrooms restrict student choice, students ask themselves "Is this all there is?" However, when we design for choice, we empower students and help them develop and take more responsibility for their own learning. Think about how much of your literacy block you are asking students to do your work versus how much time they spend doing their self-chosen work. How does this impact how students feel about the work they are doing? How often do we own the work rather than our students?

In their work Johnson and Stixrud (2018) have found that "agency may be the one most important factor in human happiness and well-being" (10). Children need opportunities to figure out what is important to them. A child who has been supported at home and at school to be self-driven does not look to other people's expectations, rewards, insecurities, or fears. Instead, they are motivated by themselves. When we support children to be self-driven in classrooms, particularly as readers and writers, they gain a sense that they have control over their own learning and in doing so are energized. When we partner with families to raise self-driven children at home and at school, we essentially vaccinate children against future depression, anxiety, and addiction. Stixrud and Johnson further explain that "we really can't control our kids—and doing so shouldn't

I Not sure I agree with that?

Students Making Choices
About Where to Write

be our goal. Our role is to teach them to think and act independently, so that they will have the judgement to succeed in school and, most important, in *life*" (4). They urge us to start with the assumption that kids have brains in their heads and want their lives to work and that, with some support, they'll figure out what to do.

Literacy researchers have been essentially advocating for the same thing. For over three decades, research on motivation (Bandura 1986; Gambrell 1996; Ivey and Broaddus 2001; Guthrie and Humenick 2004) has found that choice is widely acknowledged as a method for enhancing motivation and that students' self-concepts and the value they place on reading are critical for their success. Allington and Gabriel (2012) found that students read more regularly, understand more, and are more likely to continue reading when they have the opportunity to choose what they read. As teachers, providing choice for students not only supports their sustained happiness, it sets them up for greater success as readers and writers.

In *Mindsets and Moves: Strategies That Help Readers Take Charge*, Gravity Goldberg (2015) explains that "owning your reading means being an initiator of your own intentions as a reader" (14). Goldberg also describes what she sees as an "ownership crisis" because a lack of ownership for students is so prevalent and pervasive in classrooms. That manifests itself in students either not caring about their reading and writing lives or not applying strategies that were taught. It also manifests itself when adults make assumptions about students' lack of effort. In a reader- and writer-owned classroom, students are self-directed and make choices about their literacy learning. They choose books, reading spots, and what to work on while reading and have clear reasons why. They choose how to write about reading and how to talk about reading. They set goals for themselves rooted in the kinds of reading and writing that they care about.

What else can we do right now? We can model making our own book choices. We can make suggestions and help kids build book stacks and writing territories that will matter to them. We can trust the research and know with confidence that when children have more control in choosing what they read, they will select texts that develop their literacy skills and they will be engaged in the process. The same holds true for the need for choice in children's writing lives if we want to foster writing as a lifelong, worthwhile way to communicate with the world. There must be space for choice in regular, consistent, and predictable ways. If children can find books they love to read or genres they love to write, we can help create for students a brain state that fosters high focus, high energy, high effort, and low stress. We can show our students that we trust their inner voice so they can learn to trust in that voice, too.

Choice itself is not the end goal; rather, supporting students to be self-driven in learning and in life is the goal. So what can we design for to make authentic choice a reality in our classrooms? Design solutions often come from the simplest solution—in this case, book choice, response choice, writing choice, and illustration choice.

BOOK CHOICE

Research on book choice is clear. If we want students to read books every day mostly for pleasure, then kids need to be able to read what they want. Allington and Gabriel (2012) found in their research that above everything else that choice is perhaps the most important element of high-quality reading instruction. Yet, literacy leaders like Reggie Routman (2000) remind us that "just find a book and read" is not the pathway to designing a system of intentional, deep literacy work that is also choice driven. Choice is most powerful when it is used with purpose. So how do we support students to be self-driven in their text choices and to do so with purpose?

Book Talks

There are many ways teachers actively design instruction with choice in mind to support students to get comfortable with being self-driven. They encourage and schedule book talks led by students. In my fourth-grade classroom, we had a blank paper calendar that hung on one of the literacy bulletin boards with a pen attached on a piece of string. Each day two students could write in their initials to kick-start our day with a brief, informal book talk. They didn't need to write a paragraph or fill out a book review or graphic organizer. They simply signed up to come to the front of the classroom with a recent book they loved to tell us about it in a few brief sentences. On the days when no one was signed up, I gave a book talk on one of the books in our classroom. In doing so, I tried to rotate across genres and book formats and ensured the inclusion of picture books, graphic novels, narrative nonfiction, and informational books that I knew could capture the imaginations and interest of my students that year. I kept a running list of these book talk books so that I could notice patterns in what students chose to share about and what I had shared.

Rather than using the book talks as a space for summarizing, I wanted my students to incorporate details that helped them explain the ways the book made them think as well as what it made them feel. They needed to consider what the other members of our class as the audience would benefit from rather than what they thought I wanted to hear. There was no checklist or rubric. The book talks were not graded. Rather, they were designed to be conversational, lighthearted, and joyful sparks to start our day. Questions I posted that helped them gather their thoughts for the talk included:

What did you notice that grabbed your attention in the book?

What did the characters or topic make you think?

What did you find yourself wondering about while reading?

How did the book make you feel? Why?

Who would also enjoy this book? Why?

Think about ways you can design for book talks to be a consistent classroom routine. Perhaps they could start each school day, or they could be a weekly event that students look forward to and plan intentionally for. Consider ways you can begin the year by modeling book talks, and then invite students to give short, regular book talks about books that they want everyone to know about.

Book Clubs and Book Tasting

In Elyse's fifth-grade class, a deep and powerful book culture is alive. Every time I visit I am increasingly impressed by the students' desire to read and keep reading. Children spread themselves out across the floor, and every pair of eyes is squarely focused on the text in front of them. When Elyse facilitates book clubs in the spring, she trusts her students to choose the books that they most want to read. She does not assign book club books based on book level. Nor does she assign books based on genre. She organizes multiple copies of recently released books across genres as well as long-standing favorites her students have loved over the years. She also leads a minilesson on book selection day where she talks about how she selects books as a member of an adult book club. Her first and foremost suggestion for her students is that they look for a book that they think will surprise them or that they think will make them feel something as a result of reading the book. Elyse also knows that when her fifth graders enter middle school, they will have increased responsibilities as learners. They will need to budget their time, be more independent, and make reasoned decisions. That can be daunting if you haven't had experiences that set you up for success with these increased responsibilities. Elyse knows that the way she designs the book club experience gives her fifth graders the benefits that come from knowing the decisions they made were effective and important to them.

Elyse sets the books out for a book-tasting experience similar to a cake tasting a couple may enjoy before their wedding. Students have the length of a period to book browse, read a few pages, trade in books, and then to set out to make their book club choices. To support her students to be self-reflective, thoughtful, and responsible, she asks them to write her a letter explaining why they would like to select a particular book by responding to the questions: How do you think this book will surprise you? How are you hoping this book will make you feel? Elyse is always amazed by the insights they give her into their book selections. The book club selection is not anything goes in her classroom, rather it is intentionally designed for students to think, feel, and take action by making choices they believe will impact them.

Classroom Library Curation

As a designer at heart, the space of the classroom library was always on my mind, especially at the start of the year. I wondered to myself, *What about the library would make my students want to read beyond their comfort zones? What books did I think would make them think and feel in new ways? When it came to the physical space, how could my students have input into how our library is organized based on what matters most to them?*

Student-Created Classroom Library Bins

The first thing I did each August was take stock of my collection, taking note of books that were battered or worn out, which was often a sign they were well loved. If I had a book budget, I had to decide whether these books had more life and love in them or whether they needed to be replaced. Sometimes, I gathered these beloved books and gave them their own basket titled "Guaranteed Good Reads" so that students knew they may be a bit worn around the edges, but that's because they were loved by many other readers before them.

Sometimes I took my entire collection and made piles of related books on the classroom carpet in front of me with my trusty sticky notes in my hand for labeling. Depending on the grade level, I often ended up with bins of books based on series, characters, and authors, but I also designed names for genre bins to catch student attention. Sometimes I used the power of alliteration, so books all about animals I simply named "Amazing Animals." Books all about artists and changemakers, I labeled "Inspiring Innovators." Sometimes, I used the power of rhyme to catch their attention so books all about vehicles I labeled "Transportation Station." Sometimes, instead, I posed questions on my label, such as biographies about famous people that I titled "Hmm, . . . Just Who Will I Be?" I have a personal collection of Calvin and Hobbes books that I grouped with other humorous series books and labeled "Get Ready to Laugh Out Loud." Books that genuinely surprised me as a reader, like Kwame Alexander's *The Crossover* (2014), I put in a group labeled "Be Surprised Here." Books that made me cry or feel something really strongly I labeled "Bighearted Books." Whatever the labels, play with it. Have fun. And invite your students into the process as designers and curators by encouraging them to group books that you are unsure of or that you think they will have fun organizing by helping them use alliteration, rhyming, or questions to get readers interested in the books.

Here are some of my favorites:

Guaranteed Good Reads

Transportation Station

Amazing Animals

Inspiring Innovators

Heroes and Villains

Laugh Out Loud

Jump out of Your Seat

Be Surprised Here

Bighearted

Hmm, . . . Just Who Will I Be?

Who? What? Where? When? Why? How?

Favorite Friends

Be willing to break out of organizing books by level. Be willing to break out of traditional genre labels for bins. Be willing to engage your students in the process of designing a classroom library that makes sense for them and that sparks joyful reading. Imagine that if you were seven, ten, or twelve years old, what would entice you to want to read something new? What would help you see yourself on the shelf?

READER RESPONSE CHOICE

Offering students choice in how they respond to what they have read lets them know there is no singular reading experience or singular best way to respond. When we require that students respond in a set format, such as a five-sentence summary, we limit the kinds of cognitive and emotional responses students can have as readers. Some books make us want to tell others about them. Some books make us wish the characters were real. Some books make us want to express what we felt without having to use words. Some books inspire us to go back and reread to put the story in order as we relive the most important events. Some books leave us with more questions than answers. Supporting students to respond in a way that feels right for them based on their experience with the book means trusting students to respond in a way that's right for them at that moment.

Additionally, we always want to invite students to respond to the things they have read in ways that adult readers authentically respond to texts in the world. So how do adult readers respond to things they have read in authentic ways that can also serve as opportunities for students to think more deeply about what they read? The following ideas are designed to support students to keep reading and responding in authentic ways always with an eye toward nurturing habits of lifelong reading.

Although correspondence has become more digitized, readers in the world do write to one another to offer book recommendations. Students can craft a letter to you or a classmate that includes a bit of summary but mostly lets someone else know what the book made them think and how it made them feel.

Students can tap into their inner artist to respond by creating an original drawing, painting, sculpture, dance, or chalk art of their favorite scene from the book or by creating a work of art inspired by the story in some way. For example, as an adult some of the most moving dance pieces I have witnessed have been interpretations of works of literature or songs expressed through dance. Students may even want to respond across media, thereby transmediating their thinking.

Students could respond by reviewing the book in some creative way, either by writing a book review that mirrors the kind of reviews you might see in the *New York Times*

Book Review or the *School Library Journal* site. Students may want to explore the site Goodreads.com and offer a digital review for future readers. Finally, students may want to review a book in other digital ways by creating their own book review podcasts or YouTube video book reviews. We may have budding NPR book critics or future Mr. Shu's in our classrooms.

Research continues to show us that the more time students spend reading, the stronger readers they become. Yet, response has a place in our classrooms. When students are given time and a variety of choices in how they respond to what they've read that mirror how adults respond to books in the world, they are able to strengthen their thinking. They are able to rehearse their ideas and transfer them into a new form either by speaking, writing, or creating. They may even find that they have formed new identities as reviewers, artists, and corresponders through the process.

WRITING CHOICE

The great E. B. White said, "I admire anybody who has the guts to write anything at all"(Keyes 2003). Writers make choices every day with every word they write. And all writing is creative. Think about Charlotte poised and ready to weave just the right word into her web. She debated with herself what the right word would be, knowing that the word she chose had to have the power to save her friend, Wilbur. She decided on *Some Pig*, a phrase that would capture the

attention of the Zuckermans and would help them see Wilbur in a new way. Of course, we know it worked! Charlotte grappled with what to write each time she chose a word for her web. As a writer, she kept her audience in mind. She knew that the power of words to illuminate others could be found in a single word.

Student Comic

Every student comes to school wanting to write. Donald Graves (1983) reminds us that "this is no accident. Before they went to school, they marked up walls, pavements, newspapers, with crayons, chalk, pens, or pencils . . . anything that makes a mark. The child's marks say, 'I am'" (3). Likewise, Lucy Calkins (1986) reminds us that writing has and will continue to be a way for humans to connect and articulate their experiences:

> We need to make our truths beautiful. With crude pictographs, cave men inscribed their stories onto stony cave walls. With magic markers, pens, lipstick, and pencils, little children leave their marks on bathroom walls, on backs of old envelopes, on their big sister's homework. In slow wobbly letters, the old and the sick in our nursing homes and hospitals put their lives into print. . . . By articulating experience, we reclaim it for ourselves (3).

Think about the choices students have before they come to school to make their mark. The following sections are designed to help you expand the choices students have as writers so that they have more ways to participate and say something of meaning.

Word Choice

One of the simplest ways to inspire students to make choices as writers is to start with the smallest writing unit we have—the almighty word. In Peter Reynolds' (2018) *The Word Collector*, Jerome finds words he loves all around him. While some kids collect baseball cards, coins, or bugs, Jerome collects words. He collects two-syllable treats and simple words like *please* and *thank you*. He collects words he hears and words he sees. He strings words up on a clothesline and plays with their order. In the end, he gathers up his words and releases them into the air as gifts for others to find. This book is a great way to inspire students to be their own word collectors. Becoming a great writer can be a daunting challenge. But becoming a word collector can feel lighthearted, fun, and even easy. Writers choose every word they write, and the more words you know, the easier and more joyful that process becomes.

Students worked together to create a class reminder poster about word alternatives.

Genre/Topic Choice

Of course we want to transition students from making choices about words to sentences and full pieces that they can feel proud of creating. So how else can we design for writing choice beyond inspiring students to become word collectors? A wise mentor of mine once shared, "If I choose the genre, they choose the topic. If I choose the topic, they choose the genre." What does that look like in practice?

The units my fourth-grade students engaged in were inquiry driven and far reaching. One unit was focused on sharing the planet with emphasis on biodiversity and conservation. In the first half of the unit, I chose the genre—persuasive letters—and students chose a topic related to sharing the planet. Students also chose the letter recipients including the president of the United States, the New York City mayor, and the Environmental Protection Agency. The second half of the unit, I chose the specific topic—water conservation—and the students chose which genre they wanted to use to express what they had learned. Students created comic strips, all-about books, poetry, and even songs.

Nice idea

To whom it may concern,
My class has been studying water conservation.
Here are my ideas. Don't waste water – Take a
shorter shower or bath so it won't use too much water.
Never contaminate water. Try hard to save the water
resources. Never throw garbage in water. We've learned
about how much water we use each day. Some facts
are: a shower takes 40 gallons if you take 10 minutes,
a leakly faucet can waste 100 gallons each day, a human
body has 75% of water, less than 2% of earth's
water supply is fresh water, and an average family uses
about 88 gallons by just flushing the toilet.
Thank you for reading this letter.

Sincerely,

Shawn

As with book choice, giving your students writing choice does not necessarily mean anything goes. Like intentionally designing choice as a foundation for reading instruction, choice in writing must be intentional and purposeful. Questions to ask yourself as a starting place on your own or with your team members are: Where in the curriculum will genre choice make students more self-driven, purposeful, and happier? Where in the curriculum will topic choice make students more self-driven, purposeful, and happier? What shared experiences can we have as writers that lead up to more intentional and personal writing choices?

Some teaching points for lessons that I have found help students feel empowered to make their own writing choices include:

- Writers make purposeful choices by thinking about what medium will best communicate their message to an audience.
- Writers make purposeful choices by planning the structure to their piece.

Need to add
magazines to
Mentor Text
library

- Writers make purposeful choices that celebrate the beauty of words.
- Writers make purposeful choices as they look back at their writing and see it with new eyes.
- Writers make purposeful choices about what they like and want to keep, what to cut, and what to move.
- Writers think about the topics that make their heart sing and then take a risk and make a choice.
- Writers trust their readers to honor their choices and to respond with kindness.

ILLUSTRATION CHOICE

The world of children's literature shows us that illustrators today do not limit themselves to a tiny blank box at the top of a writing page to tell stories without words. Illustrators use a variety of media from collage to colored pencil, graphite, watercolor, oil pastel, photography, and digital rendering. They play with white space. They use a variety of panels and points of view. They use color for effect, including the absence of color. The work of illustrating is more than adding a picture; it's a process determined by the illustrator by considering the full range of techniques, materials, and possibilities available to them.

To support your students to consider the choices they have as illustrators, start by immersing them in picture books. Encourage them to linger on the page. To find illustrations that grab their attention or make them wonder. To find something that they want to try. When students are in the habit of noticing and naming what they see in books, they can shift from general observations to more specific noticings about the kinds of choices they may have themselves as illustrators. In the same way you might encourage students to notice a writer's style in an author's study, consider engaging students with an in-depth look at one illustrator to model what choices you see the illustrator using.

Classroom Spot to Make Your Mark

Once students are immersed in noticing and naming illustrators' choices and are gathering illustration mentor texts, consider creating a "Mark Maker" area or "Dialogue-Making Station" in your classroom. This is more than a writing center. This is a place for students to experiment, explore, and surprise themselves with new ways of illustrating their ideas. Include a variety of art-making materials and images from favorite classroom read-alouds to inspire the mark makers in your classroom.

Dialogue-Making Station

5 WS AND 1 H AS A GUIDELINE TO LET GO

Not knowing how to give students choice sometimes holds us back as teachers from giving choice. The simplest way to consistently and purposefully design for choice that I have found is to use the 5W1H format to help me know if I am giving enough choice or a balance of choices across the year to increase my students' happiness alongside their achievement. If we want students to be self-driven and agentive in their learning, we can support them to make choices around these basics:

Who are you reading with? On your own? With a partner?

What are you reading? Book choice!

Where are you reading? On the floor? At a desk? At a standing desk?

When are you reading? Right away? After you jot some thinking? After you book browse?

Why are you reading? What is your purpose for reading today?

How are you reading? In a book? Online? On a tablet or e-reader?

The same is true for writing:

Who are you writing for or sharing your writing with?

What are you writing? Genre choice? Topic choice?

Where are you writing? Desk? Standing desk? Out in the hall? At the window?

When are you writing? After drawing? Before drawing? After talking it out?

Why are you writing? What is your reason for writing today?

How are you writing? By hand? Using a laptop? Using a tablet?

Think about the role authentic choice plays in your classroom. What questions do you feel like you already give your students agency over? Which can you embrace to give your students more choice and agency? This 5W1H structure is designed to help you let go. The research shared is included to help you trust that letting go is the right thing to do. Dare to teach differently. Dare to make authentic choice a pillar that you intentionally design for in your classroom, and find like-minded teachers to support you in the process.

DESIGN FOR CHOICE

- Student book talks:

    What did you notice that grabbed your attention in the book?

    What did the characters or topic make you think?

    What did you find yourself wondering about while reading?

    How did the book make you feel? Why?

    Who would also enjoy this book? Why?

- Book clubs
- Book tasting
- Inviting students to label book baskets
- Reader response choice:

    Letters

    Artwork

    Performing

    Quotes

    maps

    Time lines

    Questions

    Podcast

    YouTube video

    Digital story

- Writing choice:

    Word choice

    Topic choice

    Genre choice

    Illustration medium choice

    Layout choice

- 5 Ws 1 H

Chapter 4
Challenge

> Happiness is the meaning and the purpose of life,
> the whole aim and end of human existence.
>
> —Aristotle

CLASSROOM STORY: CHOICE WORDS

On Earth Day, Amy is wearing a baseball hat embellished with colorful flowers that she carefully glued on the night before. She wears it with pride at the front of her sixth-grade class, and her students come up to her to see it up close and to ask her how she made it. The hat is memorable, and that's exactly what Amy was going for. Amy puts tremendous time and energy into catching her students' attention and trying to keep it knowing that she is competing with video games like *Fortnite* and her students' Instagram accounts. Amy strives to consider her students' strengths, their concerns, and their priorities as young people. Yet, Amy started to recognize that when she asked a question, the same students always responded. She could count on Casey, Ian, and Jonathan to have their hands up and to share a logical and thoughtful response. But conversations in class started to feel like ping-pong between her and a few predictable students, rather than volleyball with the whole class. Amy started to bravely think to herself: *I'm a good teacher, but am I good for everyone?*

In my observations over the course of several months in Amy's first-period class, students like Eleanor and Mindy often looked up from their papers and smiled, but they had yet to give an answer to a question Amy had posed to the whole class. When they worked with a small group, the same dynamic applied. Other students' voices rose to the top of the conversation while Eleanor and Mindy could often be found nodding in agreement. Amy and I wondered if they were paying attention. We wondered if they had the background knowledge to contribute to all of the questions. We wondered what the gender dynamic in class had to do with who was participating and who wasn't. We wondered if we could design our way out of this common class problem to change the dynamics of who participated.

What we were noticing about participation in Amy's class is consistent with studies on self-doubt in girls. Research has shown that self-esteem for girls peaks at nine years old. Nine! When we looked at the class dynamics, we realized that for all of the ways

Amy tried to make instruction memorable, to get her students' attention, and to motivate them as learners, it felt like some students were opting out.

We wanted to disrupt the social dynamic that had been set of some students routinely answering questions with others taking more passive roles. Amy knew she wasn't alone and this is a common problem teachers face, especially in middle school classrooms. We started to closely look at the language Amy was using in lessons and how subtle shifts could change whose voices emerged. Central to all of our phrases was one simple word—*you*. Over time, we began to categorize the statements that we tried and the impact a shift in language practices had on her students. We narrowed down our categories to four kinds of statements that grabbed her students' attention and that motivated them to participate:

Strength

One way you know you are strong is when . . .
You are strong because . . .

Appreciation

One thing I appreciate about you is . . .
You've taught me . . .

The Power of a Big Reveal

I'm going to let you in on a secret . . .
You may already knows this but . . .

Call to Action

You may be thinking to yourself . . .
Looking at your notes, you can . . .
You can get ready to . . .
You can try . . .

The first day Amy tried some of this new language, both Eleanor and Mindy's hands went up. Amy called on them without fanfare, but inside we were doing cartwheels. Changing her language choices to intentionally plan for ways to motivate her students felt new and it was working. Designing literacy instruction with a focus on motivating *all* of her students to take on their own challenges and to find their own meaning in lessons became a yearlong focus.

In *Choice Words: How Our Language Affects Children's Learning*, Peter Johnston (2004) explains that agency comes from the sense that children can tell themselves, "Yes, I imagine I can do this" when faced with a new challenge. This happens when we consistently ask our students questions like "How did you figure that out?" and "What can you try?" All of our students will experience challenges, but how we frame challenges in our literacy classrooms sets up the ways students will feel about themselves now and in the future. When motivating students to participate, to try their best, or to think in new ways, we sometimes put the onus on students. If only Max paid more attention in class . . . If Paula really cared she would . . . If Jasmin just put in more effort . . . If only Alec had more grit and determination . . . Other times we put the onus on ourselves as teachers and we search on YouTube for the most inspirational video or we try to think of the best, most motivating warm-up question to kick off the lesson. We try to be magicians and showmen.

Neither of these approaches focuses on what we know about the roots of happiness and how we can design instruction around it. As human beings we have to believe that there is the possibility we will be recognized for something positive. We have to find reasons to drive our own motivation day after day. We have to commit our attention toward the things we want to learn.

RESEARCH SAYS: ATTENTION AND MOTIVATION GO HAND IN HAND

As reported by NPR, there is a growing concern in the United States that the attention span of children is declining (Doucleff 2018). But researchers across fields are questioning whether attention is the real problem or whether what triggers our attention is more important. Our brains don't have a central place that controls our ability to pay attention and to tune out distractions. Instead, hundreds of different parts of our brains communicate and interact with one another when we pay attention. Neuroscientists have found that extra motivation increases our ability to sustain attention by more than 50 percent. In fact, it's hard to separate motivation from sustained attention. Literacy learning requires significant attention. It requires tremendous attention to learn the multiple sounds that letter combinations make, to listen to teachers modeling new reading and writing strategies, and to hear the details of a complex story read aloud. So, what motivates students to pay attention? Research from across fields is starting to look at the question of motivation and sustained attention globally. What they're finding is clear: children in other parts of the world have an enormous amount of freedom in their lives. The freedom to make decisions about their time, where they go, and what they do. As a result, children in other parts of the world are used to focusing their attention on the things that matter to them the most.

Children in Guatemala, for example, have the freedom to design their schedules and set their own agendas for their free time. Rather than having an adult set goals for them, children set them for themselves. As a result, children learn how to manage their own attention with less direction from adults. Likewise, in the Netherlands, students are given more autonomy than in most other parts of the world, there is less emphasis on obedience, and students are not burdened by the expectation of "being good." Researchers are finding in the Netherlands that when children have more freedom to drive their own decision making as learners, they learn what they like, and they grow in their social skills in the process. Like our global peers, to design for our students' happiness as much as their success, we must give ourselves permission to let go of control to increase motivation and joy.

Edward Deci and his colleagues (1975, 1995) from the University of Rochester have been studying attention for over fifty years and found that the number-one predictor of sustained attention is autonomy. To do something with the full sense of willingness and choice. So, we know that autonomy builds the self-motivation that really drives learning. But, of course, teachers can design their instruction to increase the possibility that children will become self-motivated as literacy learners so that they can grow in autonomy. Amy's shifts in language made a big difference to who felt motivated to contribute in class. So what else can we do to design our literacy instruction to increase students' self-motivation?

At the start of the school year, you might consider asking your students questions like: "What would you do if you didn't have to do anything else?" You may hear answers like fishing, playing basketball, Pokemon, bracelet making, and likely a lot about Netflix and video games. That's a barometer for what will motivate them. Then, use that information to provide links to literacy lessons. Look for read-alouds that offer connections to students' interests. Use examples and analogies that tie into these areas of interest as part of your lesson warm-up. Encourage students to make connections to the things they love as part of your lessons. Actively encourage them to write about the things they love including superheroes, wrestling, video games, and other passions that you may not share.

One year my oldest son, Jack, was told he wasn't allowed to draw a picture of wrestling, but he was allowed to draw football. Unfortunately, he didn't particularly care about football and the distinction of what counted as appropriate and what didn't seemed arbitrary. We don't have to love everything our students do, but we have to support them to tap into and come to understand the things that motivate them.

Beyond tapping into our students' interests, there's more we can do to motivate students. Students can set their own purposes for learning each day. It has become common and expected for teachers to write the lesson purpose or objective for learning on the board at the front of the classroom. Students are told what the objective is rather than having some control over what they hope to get out of it. Consider releasing some control for students to set their own purpose for learning each day by helping them narrow their focus. Can they set their own goal for listening? Can they set their own goal for speaking up when they have an idea? Can they set their own goal for starting a new book series or for writing a few more sentences than they did the day before? I'm not suggesting we abandon having our own clear and purposeful teaching objectives as educators. Those hold us accountable for the teaching we are charged with. But our purpose for teaching may not always match up with our students' individual purposes for learning that day. It takes time at the beginning of the year to set the tone that students will be setting their own purposes for learning every day. You can start by giving students an opportunity to create goals for themselves that include how they want to grow stronger every day as a learner.

> I would like to work on having more confidence and be less shy. I want to be more of a risk-taker. I mean that I want to ask for help when I'm confused more. I also want to try to learn division. I don't really get it. I am pretty good at multiplication and I like it, but I really don't understand division.

Setting Personal and Academic Goals

Think about the times you've been asked to listen to learn something and what motivated you. A simple example is to picture yourself in a professional development session where you didn't elect to be there and you're not sure whether the topic really applies to you. If the speaker doesn't grab your attention right from the start, you might take out your phone and start checking email or scrolling Facebook or Instagram to see what's new in your friends' lives. Your best friend's new baby is probably more attention grabbing than the PowerPoint you are supposed to be following. But, what if you were positioned at the start of the session to set your own purpose for being there?

Skilled listeners go into any learning environment with a sense of what they want to get out of it. When you set your own purpose for listening, you are more likely to pull yourself back into the learning when your attention starts to wander, and you'll opt out of pulling your phone out of your bag or thinking about tomorrow's lesson plans. We learn by doing. We learn by watching. We learn by listening. All of this requires the self-motivation to do so. When we release some control for students to set their own purposes for learning that day or that lesson, students are charged with finding their own reasons to be motivated to learn. This is essential, especially when lessons require more sustained attention, when texts become more complex, or when students must apply multiple strategies to hold onto story lines.

LEARNING IS AN ADVENTURE

One of the great powers we have as teachers is to create the feeling that learning is an adventure. In the book *Thing Explainer: Complicated Stuff in Simple Words*, author Randall Munroe (2015) explains how something interesting or important works using only the one thousand most commonly used words. The whole book is an adventure in learning. In the introduction he explains, "Using simple words lets me stop worrying so much. I could just have fun making up new names for things and trying to explain cool ideas in new ways." His periodic table or table of "pieces everything is made of" explains each element in a memorable and simple way such as the box for lithium says "the metal in your phone's power box." He explains the constitution in a single page in simple language including my favorite for Article VI, "Everyone, listen up." As teachers, we have a lot to learn from Munroe about how to make learning feel like an adventure by using language that motivates students to choose engagement. The key to doing this is to be interesting, understandable, and funny when we can.

So what does that look like in practice? Although as teachers we may not have control over the daily schedule, we have control over what language we use to name things to inspire, engage, and activate students. Rather than traditionally named subjects, the daily schedule can incorporate language intended to motivate students to have something to look forward to in their day: Design and Technology and Imagination Investigation. Picture in your mind gathering a group of first graders and giving them the choice of whether to go to Imagination Investigation or Writing Workshop. I know which one I would pick if I were in first grade. Another example is to picture gathering students on the rug for reading strategies. Now imagine gathering them to learn the secrets that unlock stories. Again, I know which one I would pick. Consider using language for learning across the day that sparks interest and motivation in the young learners in your care. Here are a few that may bring a smile to your students' faces:

Sample Daily Schedule

Imagination Investigation (artist/writing workshop)

Story Secrets (reading or writing workshop: narrative)

Discovery Zone (reading or writing workshop: nonfiction)

Make the Case (reading or writing workshop: opinion/persuasive)

Knowledge Quest (research)

Wordsmithing (vocabulary)

Better yet, recruit your students to help in the process of naming the kinds of learning they do, and use their language to create the schedule.

START WITH STRENGTHS

Early in my career, I mistakenly assumed challenge meant competition. Competition with oneself, table against table, and the whole class against itself. Which table will take the lead this week on stamina? Will we reach the points we need as a class to earn something extra? Who has read the most books? Although this approach may have motivated some students, it more likely caused more anxiety than inspiration. Over time, I have learned that the language we use deeply matters as to whether students will try something new, participate, or challenge themselves in new ways.

Any time we create a situation where students are comparing themselves to others, we've likely created the enemy of learning. As humans, when we compare, we tend to despair. Think about the role social media plays in your own life as an example. If you are like me, as soon as you post something—a photo of you somewhere special, an article you love, an achievement of some kind—you want to know how many likes you get. While you're waiting to see how many likes you have, you are probably scrolling to see the lives of your friends. Then, the comparing sets in, and we feel less confident than just a few minutes ago.

The only competition students should be in, especially in a literacy environment, is with themselves. We know that leveling books as a student tool, rather than a teacher tool, creates enormous competition even as early as kindergarten and that selecting books by level rather than by interest, series, author, or topic counters the goal of lifelong, intentional, joyful reading. Rather than using book levels as a metric, support students to understand that the effort they put in to their learning helps them reach new levels in themselves. Help them to know that we all have the ability to change. We all have to make choices for change to happen. We also all stumble and fall. What gets us back up is a belief that our strengths will see us through any challenges we may face.

Master storyteller and Caldecott-winning author Dan Santat knew that children need a reason to get up after the fall. He took the traditional nursery rhyme of Humpty Dumpty and reframed the narrative from one where Humpty's fall is his defeat to one where Humpty is no longer defined by his fall but by his inner strength. As explained in the blurb for *After the Fall: How Humpty Dumpty Got Back Up Again* (Santat 2014), "Life begins when you get back up." Part of what makes Santat's story so emotional is because Humpty has complexity. He has agency. We see ourselves in him. Children will make immediate connections to times when they, too, fell and got back up. But literacy learning has its own types of falls. There will be times when children will not know what to write. Or how to spell something. Or what sound those letters make. Or what that word means. Or how to say what's on their mind. Or how to respond to a question. Or how to add on to a partner's ideas. *After the Fall* can serve as a touchstone text throughout the year for students to know that they should expect to fall sometimes in literacy learning and in life. It also helps them to know that our brains grow more when we stumble and fall and get back up again.

A lot of strengths that students have are easily visible. Elementary school children immediately tend to tell me unprompted who the fastest kid is on the playground. Who can get across the monkey bars. Who is the "best" reader and "best" artist. Who is the most popular. These things seem visible to them and usually have to do with external measures of strength. One of our challenges as educators is to shift their thinking about strength to something that comes from within and that is the result of effort rather than a false sense of natural ability.

We can help students start to think about their own strengths by acknowledging that strength comes from challenge. Giving students time to reflect on their strengths through artwork and writing needs to be semiregular rather than a singular experience. Consider intentionally building a routine that you can commit to, such as the first day of every month kicking off the literacy block with a guiding question about strengths like:

September: What is a strength of mine you cannot see?

October: What am I most proud of myself for overcoming at school? At home?

November: What is a strength of mine that I am grateful for?

December: How have others helped me build my strengths?

January: What is a new strength I hope to have this year?

February: What do I love most about me? About other people in my life?

March: Who do I admire that can help me build my strengths?

April: When something is hard, how do I try again?

May: What is something new I want to try to surprise myself?

June: What can I do now that I couldn't do at the start of the school year?

Likewise, build in a routine where students have an opportunity during the wrap-up of a lesson to share what felt good in their reading or writing that day but also what felt hard. Ask wrap-up questions like:

What did you admire in yourself today (as a reader or writer)?

How did you deal with challenges today (as a reader or writer)?

What made you feel strong today (as a reader or writer)?

What did you try that you feel proud of (as a reader or writer)?

How did you help someone else become a stronger reader or writer today? How did someone else help you?

TRY SOMETHING NEW

In the Pixar film *Inside Out* (Docter et al. 2015), characters are named for the emotions we have: Joy, Sadness, Anger, Disgust, and Fear. Each character lives inside the head of a girl named Riley, but it is really the emotions that drive the story. Joy is the engine that keeps everyone moving and happy. She has a big responsibility as the center of joy for Riley. But, while she may be the most positive, she is also the least flexible. It's work for her to let go and try something new. Designing our instruction with our students' happiness in mind doesn't mean that they won't experience a range of emotions in the process. Although the primary emotion we want them to feel is joy, it's important to recognize that when we encourage them to try something new, it may stir up other core emotions. Stories help.

Remind students that we tend to admire people (and characters) more for trying than for their success. Books like *Armstrong: The Adventurous Journey of a Mouse to the Moon* by Torben Kuhlmann (2016), *The Mermaid and the Shoe* by K. G. Campbell (2014), *Frank and Lucky Get Schooled* by Lynn Rae Perkins (2016), and *It's Okay to Make Mistakes* by Todd Parr (2014) all emphasize the value of effort, trying something new, and finding your purpose. At Mount Kisco Elementary School in Mount Kisco, New York, third-grade teachers decided to read *Juana and Lucas* by Juana Medina (2016) to support their students to think about what motivates them to try something new. Juana loves lots of things: brussel sprouts, reading, playing futbol, the superhero Astroman, her home city of Bogota, Colombia, and her dog, Lucas. One thing she doesn't love is learning English. She finds it difficult and useless. When she embarks on her research to find "one single convincing reason" to learn English, she hears a variety of answers. But she has to find her own reason to try. Engaging and entertaining, Juana is a character that we admire not because she masters English by the end of the book (she doesn't) but because she is willing to change her mind and try even if it's hard.

Literacy learning asks of students the motivation to try even if something feels hard. Invite students to think about literacy learning as if they were explorers. Help them explore new ways of learning by suggesting or demonstrating a sequence of steps to reach their own goals. Help them articulate a plan, follow through, and evaluate how their plan worked after reaching their goal. Trying something new can be scary, but it's far more motivating to have support, action steps, and a chance to reflect on what worked and what didn't. One of the most important ways to motivate students to take on challenges is to simply expect that everyone will try. Not master. Not succeed. Just try. *How do we support this?*

When we build a culture of trying in our literacy classrooms, students will begin to surprise themselves. Consider creating a bulletin board that gives students a space to post how they surprised themselves. Use a variety of words that help students to be on the lookout for how they've astounded, astonished, amazed, bewildered, stunned, and even shocked themselves with the ways that they exceeded their own expectations for learning. Create a class list for all the ways we can surprise ourselves as readers and writers. Ask students questions that help them notice the ways they are surprising themselves simply by having the expectation that they will simply try something new:

RW Reflection?

- Did you read more books or pages than you thought you would have this month?
- Did you read new authors or series?
- When you look back at your writing portfolio, do you see longer sentences, more sentences, more detailed illustrations, more conventional spelling, more legible writing?
- Do you have new ways to take to the page to start a new piece?
- Do you have new ways to start a conversation? Or to keep it going?
- Do you have ways to try and retry when a word doesn't seem right?
- Do you have a new sense of confidence?
- Do you have new questions you never thought of before?

With enough practice, students can start internalizing these questions as the metric system that drives them to keep trying new things and to keep surprising themselves in the process.

Scaffolded Reading Challenge

CREATE A CULTURE OF "GO FIRST"

Think about a time when you felt your most confident. Maybe you were challenging yourself to reach new levels of you. Maybe you did something that surprised you. Maybe you look back and think *I'm glad I tried even if I failed*. One of the most powerful ways I have found for encouraging people of any age to feel motivated to challenge themselves is to build a classroom culture that inspires students to "go first." In life there are a lot of times when someone has to go first. When two people meet or have a conversation, someone has to go first. When ideas are shared in a small group, someone has to go first.

When a plan is being developed, someone has to go first. When a question is asked to a large group, someone has to go first.

Encourage students to embrace the courage it takes to go first by having them set their own "go first" challenges: Today, I will go first during partner talk/partner reading/partner writing. Today, I will go first by asking someone else "How are you?" during lunch. Today, I will go first by starting a game on the playground. Today, I will try to go first when my teacher asks a question. Today, I will go first and ask a question when I am wondering something. Today, I will go first at home by asking my family "How was your day?" before they ask me.

Some of your students may have specific literacy times of the day in mind when they want to challenge themselves to go first. But anytime students go first, they are growing in their courage and confidence. Anytime they express themselves with language by going first, they are also growing in the literacy skills associated with expression and that are necessary for speaking and listening at high levels.

Motivating students as literacy learners doesn't have to mean competition. It doesn't have to mean students have to compare themselves to anyone else. It does mean they need to be growing in autonomy, making decisions, reflecting on and using their strengths, trying something new, and challenging themselves to go first, especially so they can surprise themselves in the process.

DESIGN FOR CHALLENGE

- Plan your words carefully. Grab students' attention and motivate them to participate by honoring students' strengths, their sense of appreciation, the power of a big reveal, and by giving students ways to act:

   Strength:

   One way you know you are strong is when . . .

   You are strong because . . .

   Appreciation:

   One thing I appreciate about you is . . .

   You've taught me . . .

The power of a big reveal:

I'm going to let you in on a secret . . .

You may already knows this but . . .

Call to action:

You may be thinking to yourself . . .

Looking at your notes, you can . . .

You can get ready to . . .

You can try . . .

WW Start!

- Ask students questions like "What would you do if you didn't have to do anything else?" to understand students' varied interests.
- Rebrand the daily schedule to focus on motivation and inspiration.
- Focus on strengths throughout the year with a guiding question for each month of the year.
- Ask wrap-up questions like: "What did you admire in yourself today (as a reader or writer)?" and "How did you deal with challenges today (as a reader or writer)?"
- Inspire students to try something new and follow up by asking questions like: "Did you read new authors or series?" "Do you have new ways to start a conversation?" "Do you have a new sense of confidence?" "How?"
- Create a culture that inspires students with a "go first" challenge.

Chapter 5
Play

Life must be lived as play.

—Plato

CLASSROOM STORY: PLAY IS ALL AROUND US

In Alison's kindergarten class, she is committed to ensuring her students have a foundation in play every day. This means there is a guaranteed outdoor recess everyday, but there is also an additional choice time where students make their own choices about what they want to do with their time. There are blocks and Legos, math manipulatives, magnetic letters, and bookmaking supplies. There is a play kitchen that the children helped put together themselves with tools and minimal adult support. Off in one corner, some students are seeing what they can build with 100 cups. Thanks to visionary leadership in their school, a belief in play at every grade level has been revitalized. They host play workshops for families where grown-ups move through choice-driven stations like their children do. While adults play Twister and paddle ball, there is laughter in the air, negotiation talk about who will play what, and a spirit of collaboration and joy.

Although we may take for granted the notion that play should be a given in elementary schools, research shows this is far from the case. Psychiatrist Stuart Browne (2010) writes in his book *Play: How It Shapes the Brain, Opens the Imagination, and Invigorates the Soul* that play is like oxygen, "It's all around us, yet goes mostly unnoticed or unappreciated until it is missing." The documented decline of play for children as screen time and time spent indoors becomes more prevalent makes play in schools even more pressing at every grade level. Although open-ended play is essential, play can infuse every kind of learning students are engaged in, particularly literacy learning.

Play is not just for the early childhood years. In Chris' middle school English class, he brings play into his classroom through Shakespeare, the master of playful language. For example, Chris opens his lessons with knock-knock jokes because we owe *Macbeth* (Act 2, scene 3) for "Knock, Knock. Who's there?" Chris knows that by middle school the only "play" that tends to be valued is "competitive play." Chris knows that his students are engaged in all kinds of play including art, music, movies, comedy, flirting, and daydreaming. His classes are structured around a belief that language is meant to be playful more than anything else. Chris helps his students channel their inner Shakespeare by recognizing as writers that when language is playful, you are more persuasive because you have the attention of your audience. Likewise, he carefully plans what he says in his lessons knowing that if his language is playful, he has a greater chance his students will be smiling. He asks himself questions like, "Can I use a metaphor, simile, or turn of phrase to grab students' attention early in the lesson?" He knows that when his language choices are playful, his students will be more eager to try something new and to tackle increasingly complex texts.

Thanks to researchers and advocates, we know that the "work" of childhood is play. Through play children build their imaginations, learn how to problem solve, and navigate social networks face-to-face. Yet throughout our lives, it is through play that we learn how to move beyond frustration. When we are engaged in play we learn to use language, both verbal and nonverbal, to express our feelings, opinions, ideas, and needs. It is also through play that our minds wander and where we discover own dreams and beliefs. Above all, play creates joy, which is its own best reward. All learning, but literacy learning specifically, is ripe with opportunities for play.

When we read aloud books like *The Day the Crayons Quit* (Daywalt 2013) or *The Book with No Pictures* (Novak 2014), we create instant joy, and children (and adults) can't help but laugh out loud. We also model how authors play with language and the space of the page, which broadens our imaginations. When we read fictional books like *The Most Magnificent Thing* by Ashley Spires (2014) and *Iggy Peck, Architect* by Andrea Beaty (2007) or narrative nonfiction books like *Mesmerized: How Ben Franklin Solved a Mystery That Baffled All of France* by Mara Rockliff (2015), the characters model for students the ways they, too, can connect information they know and build something new with it again and again—an increasingly vital skill.

Think about the times when literacy learning feels playful in your classroom. I can guarantee it's when students are connecting with one another. Think about when your students are laughing at the same inferences an author has made (check out "Cookies" from Lobel's (1972) *Frog and Toad Together* for a good laugh) or when they are leaning in together to see the details an illustrator has crafted on the page. You might even say that in those moments it feels like time stands still, and you can almost see the memories being formed. When I am observing classrooms, I use a variety of engagement inventories including a play inventory. I look for signs of playfulness in the learning process: students' smiles, laughter, peer interaction, problem solving, and decision making. When there is a lot of observable, measurable evidence in these areas, you know that play is a part of learning.

RESEARCH SAYS: LEARNING FROM LEGO ABOUT FLOW

The Lego Foundation (2018), leaders in play, have found five characteristics that explain when learning through play happens: the activity is (1) joyful; (2) helps you find meaning in what you are doing or learning; (3) involves active, engaged, minds-on thinking; (4) involves iterative thinking (experimentation, hypothesis testing, etc.); and (5) involves social interaction. You might be thinking Lego has some stake in selling more Star Wars Lego kits, but a Cambridge University project saw that when children devised, told, and acted out stories with Legos before writing them down, it boosted students' narrative and writing skills, as well as interaction and cooperation. Imagine the stories our students would write if they got to build first either as a narrative warm-up or as a way to develop their stories. In my second-grade classroom, we had Lego bins with loose parts that students used to create cities and imaginary worlds. Now with Lego minifigures, students can add characters to a setting they have created themselves, sparking dialogue, conflict, and resolutions. The Cambridge Study Centre is now looking into how early play relates to other aspects of young children's development, exploring what happens to the brain during play, and is conducting a longitudinal study examining what promotes children's playfulness and how it helps learning and well-being.

Play is powerful because it naturally harnesses a set of principles that lead to learning. Play in which children lead but adults support is an especially powerful pedagogy for learning. Playful learning happens through joyful interactions. It activates iterative thinking and an engaged brain. And it harnesses social interaction.

When learning feels playful, we don't want it to end. Mihaly Csikszentmihalyi (1990) calls that experience a state of *flow*. Children engage in flow every time they play. In his follow-up work on flow and sports with coauthor Susan Jackson (1999), he writes, "Happiness is not something that happens to people but something that they make happen" (824). When I watch my youngest son, Matthew, building with Legos, drawing pictures of Angry Birds, or creating a castle out of cushions, he's in a state of flow. Not only is he self-driven through his play, but he is conditioning his brain to associate intense enjoyment with highly focused attention, practice, and hard work. His body is connected to his mind through a hands-on, minds-on approach to self-directed learning through play.

What does that look like in a classroom? We see students in a state of flow when they are transferring knowledge they've gained from a nonfiction text into something new by making their own website, public service announcement, petition, or persuasive letter. We see students in a state of flow when they are writing stories they care about not just from their own lives but from their unlimited imaginations. We see students in a state of flow when they are in book clubs where they have been empowered to choose the texts, how to respond, where to gather, and how they are going to share their reactions to the text with the class. When in a state flow, humans are at their happiest. The more easily a person can find things in life where they can get in a state of flow, the happier that person is likely to be day after day.

Our challenge is to create that experience for students every day as literacy learners by making their reading, writing, speaking, listening, and creating lives feel joyful and purposeful. We see students in state of flow when children are buried in their books in what Atwell (2007) termed the "reading zone." Or when students ask for a few more minutes to keep writing or when they groan at the end of a read-aloud because they can't wait to hear what happens next. In early childhood settings, we tend to see play valued because children are given time and space to explore, experiment, try, fail, and try again— or at least they should be if school leaders and educators are following research.

At a school I visited in London, the students had set up a potion station where they could mix concoctions and where they were encouraged to talk about what they were making to grow in their language. In the after-school lit club I run, I always bring letter tiles and the children make words when they need a break or when they have extra time. In spring, I bring sidewalk chalk and we go outside to leave inspirational messages for members of the school community. In these settings, children have opportunities to create things with their hands that are reality-inspired but also completely imaginative. They are free to gather with their peers in impromptu groupings or to play alone. Yet, that freedom associated with play often disappears the older students get. Creating a class-room environment that retains play as a core tenet of instruction helps students associate literacy learning with joy and purpose.

PLAY LEADS TO PRACTICE, MASTERY, AND RECOGNITION

In addition to simply sparking joy, intentionally designing instruction with play as the foundational core helps students build lifelong skills. A student who has many opportunities to play will quickly learn the power of practice. Practice is fundamental to becoming a strong literacy learner. Many children benefit from repeated practice to master the connection between the symbols on the page we call letters and the multiple sounds they make to become proficient readers. Many children, likewise, benefit from repeated practice to master the fine motor skills needed to form letters with automaticity. Many children benefit from repeated practice with sentence frames to feel confident sharing their ideas with others. In many ways, literacy learning thrives on repeated practice. When we connect all types of learning through hands-on, repetitive experiences, we support our students to better remember what was learned. A sequence of

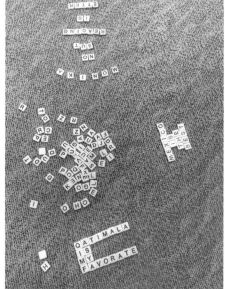

Making Words from Letter Tiles

purposeful actions is easier to recollect than random acts, and even better when combined with social (discussion) and emotional engagement.

We all know, though, that learning anything can be frustrating in the beginning—riding a bike, playing an instrument, becoming a soccer goalie, swimming on your own, learning a new language. We all have those experiences where we doubted whether the practice was worth it. Yet, if learning is so hard, why do we all do it over and over again throughout our lives? Practice becomes self-motivating if you have experience knowing that you have to go through a stage of uncertainty and possibly failure before moving into a stage where you feel you are strong enough. With encouragement, you keep trying

Everything is hard before it's easy

until you see improvement. So much of literacy learning happens with "invisible practice." That is, all of the reading, writing, speaking, listening, and creating students do when no one is watching. When we support students to read at home by sending home book baggies filled with a range of books they've chosen, we can emphasize the value of invisible practice. It's the practice you do when no one else is looking that often matters most. For children to *choose* to practice, they must have ownership of their own learning by making choices about what they read and what they write. A classroom that feels play-driven makes practice more attainable, appealing, and self-driven for students.

There are even more benefits of play. With enough steady practice and improvement over time, we experience the feeling of mastery. That's when you hear students saying, "I did it!" or "I can do it on my own!" or my favorite, "Watch this!" When we reach the point of mastery, we want to recreate that feeling again and again. Ed Hallowell (2003) explains in his book *The Childhood Roots of Adult Happiness* that the roots of self-esteem are not actually praise but in the feelings we create in ourselves through mastery. He explains, "With mastery comes not only self-esteem but also confidence, leadership skills, initiative, and an enduring desire to work hard" (7). As teachers, we can be on the lookout for "watch this" moments in our students, especially from those students that might now seek out recognition verbally.

Conferring with students is the best way I know to support them through recognition. Pulling up alongside a student for a one-on-one moment can also be playful. When we take the time to ask students about their weekend or we share something funny that happened to us that reminded us of them, we strengthen our connections with our students and are able to leverage that feeling to support students with the skills and strategies they need to master new content so that they know recognition in the form of compliments is warranted.

Recognition comes from the feeling of mastery and approval from someone outside yourself. When a child realizes they can use letters to make words, they may rush to write everything they want to say. When a child has the words to describe what they see in illustrations, they'll want to talk about everything they see with as many people as possible. It's up to us to say, "I see you and others should, too!" The best way to see students routinely and consistently is to design for it. As a classroom teacher, I photocopied a stack of class lists at the beginning of the year and labeled them with different moments of the day so I could check off moments of recognition when they occurred. Michael gave the final share during reading workshop. Check. Ada shared during writing workshop. Check. Angel shared a favorite poem from the classroom library during morning meeting. Check. This gave me a quick method for keeping track of the recognition data for my class so that I could know rather than guess at who was being recognized and for what.

In literacy classrooms, we love the power that comes from practice, mastery, and recognition. Yet, practice without play is arduous. And when we stop practicing, mastery feels unattainable and we may even start to believe we aren't capable or worthy of mastery. Likewise, recognition without play can become pressured. Then, what happens? We stop seeking recognition, or we make choices because of the recognition we gain, not because our choices bring us joy or sustained happiness.

Yet, when our classrooms are rooted in play, with time committed for students to play with ideas, with one another, and with materials, we build a wheel of happiness through our methods that allows for play-practice-mastery-recognition cycles to continuously happen. So how do we design our instruction so that play is a core ingredient for student success and happiness? Think of *experimentation* as a synonym for play, especially in literacy learning. After all, children use the same processes as scientists when they are engaged in play. They come up with a theory, test the theory to see if it fits what's observed and what others tell them, ask questions, and make predictions. Sounds an awful lot like what we do as readers as well. Now imagine what students can "experiment" with during your literacy block as a way to play. Students can play with different book choices especially when we recognize that not every book selected has to be finished. Students can play with genres until they find the one that best suits their needs for expression. Students can play with partnerships by having varied partnerships for varied purposes. Students can play by becoming characters in a story and creating their own scenes through writing, acting, and set design. Students can play with poetry by experimenting with different sounds, line breaks, and the use of white space. Students can play by using their hands to create something that shows what they learned or what they enjoyed about what they read.

PLAYING WITH IDEAS

What do you do when you are stuck finding an idea? When you are staring at the blank page? Or when you are searching for the words to say what you want to say? These are common challenges for any literacy learner, writer, or creator. Author and illustrator Philip Stead's (2016) *Ideas Are All Around* helps remind us that sometimes the best strategy is to take a look around. In first-person voice, Stead introduces his problem: "I have to write a story today. That is my job. I write stories. But today, I don't have any ideas." Stead's shaggy dog, named Wednesday, knows what's best, and together they set off on a walk around the neighborhood. Along the way they run into objects, animals, and people. In the end, Stead is ready to "take a walk on the page." Through mixed-media illustrations and playful moments in the story, the book represents a celebration of ideas.

Students can grow stronger in their thinking by intentionally designing for students to play with ideas:

- Have students take photographs of things in the classroom, in the school, or in their community to come back and write about them.
- Go on a listening walk for students to tap into their senses and to jot down what they hear as seeds for further writing.
- Use images of famous works of art and have students choose their favorite to start a list about what they see, think, and wonder to spark further writing.
- Use shared writing to create a fictional conversation between two unlikely friends as a class—think Frog and Toad, Peach and Blue, Elephant and Piggie.
- Students can use watercolors to paint their dreams and then use their paintings as seeds for writing.
- Students can write character sketches of people in their lives and what they love about them.
- Students can write about what their community may have been like long ago.

In addition to Heart Map

PLAYING WITH MATERIALS

Research from the UnLonely Project, part of the Foundation for Art and Healing, is starting to show us that artistic expression can help heal the loneliness associated with modern life. While we are technologically intertwined, we are living in a curiously isolating cultural moment. Jeremy Nobel, founder of the UnLonely Project, writes, "More people on the planet than ever before, more digitally connected than ever before, lonelier than ever before. What's going on?" (Yaffe 2018). As students get older and more digitally connected, this becomes even more urgent as they start to wonder whether they have a "click-worthy brand." Students that are already crafting a public persona that isn't really who they are find that it becomes harder for them to relate to who they are and to connect with other people.

Yet, Nobel has found that playing as a part of the creative process can counter feelings of social isolation and the fear of rejection that can diminish sustained happiness. When we are engaged in creating something, we direct our focused attention to a moment of experience. Next, we reflect on the meaning of that experience. Finally, we forge new human connections when we share that meaning with another person. Nobel's work started out focused on children who experienced trauma and illness, veterans returning from war, and survivors of national traumas. Yet, what he has found is that creative expression can enhance the life of anyone.

To support students to see themselves as creators, it takes some intentional designing that is rather simple. Construction paper, markers, scissors, paint, oil pastels, even recyclable bottles, cardboard, and paper scraps can be sources of creativity that spark stories, conversations, and innovative thinking that students design themselves. When we invite students to play with materials in new ways as creators, we invite creativity but also the opportunity for social connection.

To support students to play with materials in new ways, turn to the work of illustrators that are breaking new ground in the world of children's literature through their innovative techniques. Look to the Caldecott winners from the last ten years as a starting place:

- 2018: *Wolf in the Snow*, by Matthew Cordell (2017)
- 2017: *Radiant Child: The Story of Young Artist Jean-Michel Basquiat*, by Javaka Steptoe (2016)
- 2016: *Finding Winnie: The True Story of the World's Most Famous Bear*, by Lindsay Mattick (2015), illustrated by Sophie Blackall
- 2015: *The Adventures of Beekle: The Unimaginary Friend*, by Dan Santat (2014)

- 2014: *Locomotive*, by Brian Floca (2013)
- 2013: *This Is Not My Hat*, by Jon Klassen (2012)
- 2012: *A Ball for Daisy*, by Chris Raschka (2011)
- 2011: *A Sick Day for Amos McGee*, by Philip C. Stead (2010), illustrated by Erin E. Stead
- 2010: *The Lion & the Mouse*, by Jerry Pinkney (2009)

As students closely read the illustrations in these books, they will realize that their imaginations are limitless and that illustrators use a wide variety of methods to make their stories resonate with readers. Give students permission to play with materials by giving students paper choice and giving them the freedom to design their own illustrations using a variety of available materials. Limiting students to a particular paper with particular text boxes for illustration limits the imaginative possibilities that live inside each student. Put out a variety of materials and give students illustrated picture books as mentor texts. Encourage students to notice and name what they see and to try something in their own work that they admire.

In their book *Purposeful Play: A Teacher's Guide to Igniting Deep and Joyful Learning Across the Day*, authors Kristine Mraz, Alison Porcelli, and Cheryl Tyler (2016) explain that play is intensely personal but that we can leverage the power of play by providing a range of open-ended materials including cardboard boxes, loose parts, shells, rocks, and fabric. When children explore these materials in new ways, not only do they ignite their imaginations, they grow in their empathy for one another as they negotiate, study their classmates' faces and bodies, and learn to understand emotions. They collaborate, communicate, and grow in their capacity to try new things, fail, and try again.

Or go one step further as Suzanne Farrell Smith recommends in *The Writing Shop: Putting "Shop" Back in Writing Workshop* (2019), by reclaiming writing workshop as a method that draws from its namesake—the shops of craftspeople like carpenters, quilters, visual artists, architects, or cooks. In these shops, materials convey the message. Suzanne explains how she inspires students to tap into their inner craftsperson by showing them photographs of different kinds of workshops. She ignites their senses by offering a variety of scents for students to engage with in little glass jars (in the cleverly named "scenter"). She also gathers physical materials like objects and fabrics for students to draw inspiration from, but she also seeks out recorded sounds from nature and city streets for students to listen to as sparks for stories. She invites students to use a variety of writers' and artists' tools to take to the page including scraps of this and that, handheld audio-recording devices, and whiteboards. Suzanne explains that while the technical skills of writing should be valued and are strengthened when we return writing workshop to its name-sake—the shop. A true writing workshop offers much more than technical expertise: "Self-awareness, impulse control, seeking help, listening carefully, cooperation, conflict negotiation, appropriate risk-taking, grit, initiative, courage, consideration of the health and well-being of others: all are taught and reinforced particularly well in a shop setting" (27). Giving students invitations to play with materials in a shop setting allows students to tap into their sensory selves, to embrace the mess, and to discover something new about writing and about themselves.

LETTING STUDENTS GROW

When children are positioned as trustworthy and agentive, they grow in their confidence and willingness to try new things. We see this when students are positioned to make book choices, and they then grow in their skills and use of strategies because they are invested in understanding what they are reading. We see this when children are encouraged to write from the heart and from their imaginations giving equal value to different ways of telling and writing stories. We see this when children are not given immediate answers to their questions but when they are prompted to grow with questions described by Jan Burkins and Kim Yaris (2016) in *Who's Doing the Work? How to Say Less So Readers Can Do More*: How do you know? What does that make you think? What can you try? And how can you find out?

When we embrace the power of play, it becomes easier to recognize the countless opportunities that students have every day to grow. But sometimes we need a push to let go to let students grow. Families also benefit from support from teachers on ways to increase play at home to let children grow. The Let Grow Project is dedicated to this idea and offers families dozens of possibilities for students to do on their own or with minimal support from adults, including make a sandwich by yourself, cook breakfast for your family, play outside on your own or with a friend, ride your bike down the street, create a game from scratch. These small moments have big results. Namely, that children become problem solvers and idea generators and they learn they can make decisions that empower them. Once a Let Grow project takes root, play becomes more routine as children realize there is much they *can* do. As a part of the Let Grow project, families can take photos of their child in these Let Grow Moments and together they can write captions. Students can then share their project with their classmates, and they benefit from listening to the projects of their friends. When this becomes a movement in your school community, everyone benefits. These small things children choose to do often create big changes over time.

Of course, in some homes, children don't have a choice about their independence. They are growing constantly because they are responsible for taking care of younger siblings. They are changing diapers, making meals, and doing laundry. When children are responsible for many things in their lives for their own well-being and the well-being of others, it makes play in school even more necessary for children to be free to explore their imaginations and grow in other ways. Having play at the center of literacy learning happens most profoundly when things are new, when the student doesn't understand how something works, or when the evidence isn't clear. That's when students are willing to experiment, try, and discover something new. Having a spirit of play in your literacy class-room doesn't mean that you need a special cart that you wheel out for playful moments. Every lesson every day is an opportunity to bring a playful spirit into the work students do.

DESIGN FOR PLAY

Create a classroom that infuses play every day by trying some specific techniques:

- Play with texts:

  Use interactive picture books like Hervé Tullet's *Say Zoop!* (2017), wordless picture books like *Lines* by Suzy Lee (2017), and books with unexpected twists like *The Book of Mistakes* by Corinna Luyken (2017) and *Are We There Yet?* by Dan Santat (2016) to invite readers to play with books in new ways.

  Invite students to rewrite texts from their own lenses—what would they change?

- Play together:

  Encourage flexible partnerships and small groups that allow for impromptu and relevant conversations to happen.

  Commit to daily turn-and-talk opportunities every lesson.

  Incorporate closure to lessons and the day by providing space for students to share what felt good, what felt hard, and what they learned.

- Play with language:

  Channel your inner Shakespeare and use metaphors, similes, and stories to create a playful tone.

  Encourage students to use playful language in their writing to grab the attention of their audience.

- Play with materials:

Open up the choices students have for self-expression and invite students to use crayons, colored pencils, torn paper, watercolors, acrylic paint, digital tools, Legos, and other building materials to represent what they have learned.

Offer paper choice for student writing with various landscape/portrait options, line space, and art space.

- Play with ideas:

Create a "culture of experimentation" by fostering idea generation and risk taking.

Read aloud books that spark new thinking about where ideas can be found like:

Bear Has a Story to Tell and *Ideas Are All Around* by Philip Stead (2012, 2016);

Wild Ideas: Let Nature Inspire Your Thinking by Elin Kelsey (2015);

The Artist Who Painted a Blue Horse by Eric Carle (2011);

Frederick by Leo Leonni (1967);

and *Sky Color* by Peter Reynolds (2012).

- Read aloud books with dynamic characters who push beyond themselves to make the world more socially just and kind like:

Everyone Can Learn to Ride a Bicycle by Chris Raschka (2013);

The Most Magnificent Thing by Ashley Spires (2014);

Emmanuel's Dream by Laurie Ann Thompson (2015);

Drum Dream Girl by Margarita Engle (2015);

Trombone Shorty by Troy Andrews (2015);

What Do You Do with a Problem? by Kobi Yamada (2016);

and *Ruby's Wish* by Shirin Yim Bridges (2002).

Chapter 6
Story

> The most powerful
> words in English are,
> "Tell me a story."
>
> —Pat Conroy

CLASSROOM STORY: STORYTELLERS INSIDE US

Stories are the heart of Lina's first-grade classroom. When I walk in one afternoon to read a story to the class, I talk to six boys who are deeply immersed in Legos. One boy is flying a Lego jet he built and is making *whoosh* noises around the room. Two boys are building a tower and talking about who will live there and who might invade. Three girls and one boy are in a bookmaking station they've created themselves. They've self-selected into partnerships to draw and write stories for each other as gifts. One boy is in a story corner surrounded by tools to help him write his story so that others can read it. He tells me, "I can write really long stories, you know." He shows me his most recent story about a waterslide and another about bike riding. In Lina's classroom stories live on paper. But, stories also live in the Lego area. They live in the storytelling voices of children building with blocks. They live in students' imaginations as they create other worlds and invent new characters.

This chapter is all about how we can design our instruction so that children come to learn that they have a storyteller inside of them. There are certainly academic reasons why this is important. When children have a strong foundation in narrative and how stories work, they are able to devote brain power to the important nuances of stories that help us deepen our understanding. Yet, the outcomes of a story-centered classroom are about more than academics. When children know that they have the capacity to tell stories in a myriad of ways, they grow in their confidence, curiosity, and courage. They build a narrative about themselves that says *I am worthy. I belong.*

Compliment Wordle

RESEARCH SAYS: HARDWIRED FOR STORIES

Our brains are hardwired for stories. Research out of Stanford University has shown that stories can be up to 22 times more memorable than facts alone. That means that when stories are leveraged not only in literacy instruction but in math, science, social studies, and other content areas, students are better able to remember important content and procedures. Think about the genius of Mrs. Frizzle from the Magic School Bus series (Cole 1986) who taught generations about water, the weather, and rock formations. With her hallmark outfits and radiating positivity, Mrs. Frizzle is an unforgettable character who makes science come alive by using narrative devices that stick in our brains.

But there are many reasons why a foundation in stories is about more than strengthening comprehension. Research in neuroscience shows us that stories change our attitudes, beliefs, and behaviors. If I want a more compassionate class, the most important thing I need to do is to make sure the stories I share model what it means to be compassionate, particularly when it's hard to do so. If I want my students to be altruistic and to think of others, I read *Those Shoes* by Maribeth Boelts (2009), and I try not to cry when Jeremy leaves his black shoes with three white stripes on his classmate's doorstep when he knows he needs them more. Then I read *Wings* by Christopher Myers (2000) and let my students talk about the bravery of the characters and how hard that can be when the rest of your social world stands against you. Research across fields has found that when we hear, view, or read stories, we show greater kindness, we cooperate better with others, we are more empathetic, and we understand how others are likely to react in a situation. In this way, stories are like medicine for the soul. In *Minds Made for Stories: How We Really Read and Write Informational and Persuasive Texts*, Tom Newkirk (2014) explains that humans need stories because we crave to understand causality. If we don't have it, the world can feel chaotic, random, dangerous, and even terrifying. We seek to know why things happen, and for this we need stories.

In his book *The Storytelling Animal: How Stories Make Us Human* Jonathan Gottschall (2013) writes, "We are, as a species, addicted to stories. Even when the body goes to sleep, the mind stays up all night telling itself stories" (xiv). It's true. Our dreams are our bodies' way of continuously telling stories that blend reality with fantasy as a way for our brain to process our lives. As humans, we are built to be storytelling creatures. When our storyteller self is fueled with strategies for getting even stronger at understanding and creating stories, we are happier and more successful in the process.

Over the years, I've learned that one of the most important reminders I tell myself almost daily is that we all love someone and we all struggle with something. Understanding those basic ideas makes you more open to listening to the stories of others and makes you more willing to share your own story. When our students are conditioned by rich and powerful stories to be on the lookout for who characters love and what they struggle with, they are able to make their own stories that much more powerful in the process.

The art and science of storytelling is rooted in the ability to inspire, motivate, and, ultimately, to persuade others to take action. Some of the world's best storytellers share one other common trait—they've faced hardship and are eager to share the lessons they've learned. Great storytellers have struggled in life and have turned their adversity into something meaningful to move others to action. Challenges, failures, adversity—this is what makes stories more interesting. As human beings, we are hardwired to attend to stories of struggle that have turning points and hopeful endings.

Children intuitively know the value of stories. When you watch a group of children in any context gather around someone telling a story, they are typically mesmerized. This is physiologically rooted in our DNA. The greatest classroom management technique is to pick up a story and to start reading or to tell a story from your own life. Stories told around the classroom rug or the playground or at the town square have the same effect that stories did thousands of years ago around a campfire. Storytelling triggers imagination, creates bonds between groups of people who don't know each other, and conveys information.

Anthropologists have understood that fire was the spark that led to human evolution. However, only recently have anthropologists begun studying one of the most impactful benefits of fire—the ways coming together sparked our imaginations as humans through storytelling. With more time in the day, thanks to light from fire's flames, conversation turned from survival stories to stories that incorporated humor and adventure. The art of storytelling was born. Social anthropologists believe storytelling made up 80 percent of the fireside conversations of our ancient ancestors. Storytelling thousands of years ago in many ways served the same purposes of today. According to University of Utah anthropology professor Polly Wiessner, "Stories told by firelight put listeners on the same emotional wavelength, elicited understanding, trust, and sympathy, and built positive reputations for qualities like humor, congeniality, and innovation" (Gallo 2016, 3).

Fireside stories might have started 400,000 years ago, but our brains are still wired for stories today. Of course, the stakes have changed. According to Princeton University neuroscientist Uri Hasson, "A person who tells compelling stories can actually plant ideas, thought, and emotions into a listener's brain. The art of storytelling is your most powerful weapon in the war of ideas" (Gallo 2016, 4). When students know what stories work and why they work, their ideas are more memorable and impacting. The children in our classrooms that have a foundation in the power of stories will be able to capture the public's imagination in unprecedented ways. The more children understand the classic components of a great narrative, the more their audience will be moved to action by their ideas. Think about the power of fund-raising campaigns, commercials, and TED Talks. When a compelling story grabs hold of our attention, we are more likely to support a cause financially or by volunteering. We are more likely to purchase a product that fits into a narrative about ourselves we are trying to create. And we are more likely to go out and tell others about this amazing thing we heard. Children who understand the secrets of great stories will better be able to support others to listen and do something (hopefully, to make the world a better place).

THE SECRETS OF GREAT STORIES

Great stories that capture our attention tend to have certain things in common: sets and surprises, heroes and villains, adversity and hope, tension and triumph. This can be streamlined to three distinct steps to purposeful, powerful storytelling:

- Grab your listener's attention with a question or unexpected challenge. (Challenge)
- Give listeners an emotional experience by telling a story around a struggle that will ultimately lead to success. (Struggle)
- Galvanize listeners with a call to action. (Hope)

This is directly related to what researchers have found about working memory. Decades ago researchers found that the human mind is only capable of remembering three to seven items in a short-term, or "working," memory. People think in patterns, and three is the lowest number of units that can establish a pattern or progression. Think about common groupings of three: "Lights, camera, action"; "Ready, set, go"; "Stop, drop, and roll"; "Life, liberty, and the pursuit of happiness." In stories, we also have memorable groups of three: the three little pigs, the three bears, and three musketeers. The rule of three makes any story more effective because audiences are more likely to recall the content. A rule of three for powerful storytelling or narrative writing in your classroom could be: "challenge, struggle, hope" or "trigger, transformation, life lesson." In the early grades, this often becomes beginning, middle, and end, but students sometimes struggle knowing how to make those three parts of a story more powerful.

There are countless examples of impacting storytellers using a three-part formula to make their stories stronger. Although he was a controversial figure, it is hard to discount the impact Steve Jobs made on the modern world. In 2005 he gave a commencement address at Stanford University composed of 2,250 words in fifteen minutes (Jobs 2005). It was a classic three-part narrative with one central theme: Do what you love. Find what makes your heart sing. When you view the speech, your mind holds onto the message because of the three-part structure that our brains can process with ease. If he had deviated from that structure or had more than one compelling theme, our minds would wander, we would stop listening, and his message would not resonate. Steve Jobs was known for asking people a question that triggered storytelling, "What makes your heart sing?" The answer is different than the answer to the question "What do you do?" or "What do you love?" Steve Jobs made computers; building tools to help people unleash their creativity made his heart sing.

The singer-songwriter Sting had a specific writing process for developing his record-breaking music (Gallo 2016). He would start by listing names of people he'd known, and they would become characters in a kind of three-dimensional drama. His songs would explain who they are, what they do, and their hopes and fears for the future. It was a three-part recipe for making his listeners connect again and again.

In her famed career as an interviewer, Oprah recognized that her job was not to be an interviewer or talk show host. Rather, she described her work as about raising the level of consciousness and connecting people to ideas (Gallo 2016). That sounds a lot like the role of a teacher to me. Our role as educators is much like Oprah's in that the most impactful teachers I know inspire students to identify their life's core purpose. Oprah has told countless stories to help people understand their own life story by sharing stories of her challenges, struggles, and success using the same three-part framework.

Designing for stories to be the heart of your literacy instruction takes intentional planning to ensure that all students have access to powerful stories as they develop their own storyteller self.

STORIES ARE EVERYWHERE

One of the most important ways to start making stories a pillar of your literacy instruction beyond a single unit is to help students realize that stories are everywhere. They have stories that happen in the hallways and at their lockers. Playground stories. Walking to school stories. Bus riding stories. Sibling stories. When they talk to their friends, they are usually telling stories. "Yesterday, I _____" and "One time _____." When students realize that stories are everywhere, they are easier to listen and look for and easier to replicate on paper. By telling their own short stories to someone else or by writing or drawing different kind of stories, students build up a repertoire of stories that can turn into longer pieces over time.

Here are some quick story starters to get students talking, writing, drawing, and sharing:

- A time I was really happy (sad, annoyed, elated, surprised, proud, confused)
- A time I was upset by someone else
- A time I lost something (maybe it was found)
- A time I wished something were different
- A time I was changed
- A memory I have is _____
- The first time I _____
- The last time I _____
- What if . . .? (the question behind all fiction)

An important way to get your students comfortable with sharing stories is to share your own. When we tell stories from our own lives, students lean in to listen. You can also share the stories you are creating together by reflecting on your story as a class: "Remember the time that we . . ." Students love to hear stories where they are one of the central characters where they showed flexibility, bravery, compassion, or understanding.

The more practice students have telling stories to each other, the better they will be able to add craft to their stories such as dialogue and internal thinking. As the year goes on, you can encourage students to challenge themselves to add something new to the story they tell such as:

- something you said
- something you were thinking or wondering
- a noise or sound word
- purposeful repetition of phrases.

The more practice students have with these skills in low-stakes ways, the better able they will be to identify them in the books they read and to apply them in the stories they write or perform.

When students realize that stories are everywhere, they also learn that their own story matters. Writing about oneself and our personal experiences—and then rewriting your own story—can lead to improved happiness. We all have personal narratives that shape our view of ourselves and the world. Stories, whether real or imagined, tend to be about the same human endeavors: the quest to understand who we are, where we are from, who we will be, and what we imagine. To support students to understand the common threads of stories that undergird great literature, songs, films, or any other storied work, I have developed story frames that help students understand that telling or writing a story does not have to be hard. Oftentimes, the simpler the message, the more it will resonate with your readers and listeners. The appendix has several examples of story frames to try with your students as invitations for them to think about their own lives or to create something fictional by thinking about the things stories have in common. Writing as a way to understand who we are, where we are from, who we want to become, and what we can imagine is powerful, purposeful work that never really stops. The story frames are designed as a tool to help you get to know your students and their stories and as a way for students to take to the page as storytellers in a myriad of meaningful ways.

WHAT'S THE STORY HERE? IMAGE READING

One of the simplest ways to spark a storyteller voice in students is to have a daily image to talk about. It can be an image from a recent read-aloud, an image of children the same age as your students engaged in something joyful, or a compelling photograph of somewhere you've been or of a landmark site. When the image is character driven, it can spark discussion about what the character might be thinking, feeling, or saying. Students get to imagine the life of the character beyond the photo as they develop their storyteller voice. When the image is setting driven, it can spark discussion about what students see, what it makes them think, and what it makes them wonder. Any image can be used to imagine other sensory details like smells and sounds that we can't see but we can invent. When images are used as a foundation in understanding stories, students are given a primer in the craft techniques that will soon make their verbal and written stories that much stronger.

Some of my favorite images to share with students come from my own life, especially my childhood and my children's childhoods. I also have my favorite picture book images that I project on a Smart Board or make enlarged copies of for us to talk about how pictures work, but more importantly so that students can ask themselves "What's the story here?" The *New York Times* has a weekly "What's Going On in This Picture?" image that invites students to create their own captions for what they see. Students around the world can join a moderated conversation to see what other students come up with. In his middle school English class, my husband, Chris, had a weekly caption contest much like the *New Yorker*'s where he posts an image and students are invited to create a caption for it. Students are eager each week to know what everyone wrote and who Chris thought had the winning caption. Building a routine around image viewing does not have to take up much class time, but it helps activate student's narrative selves in a quick, deeply beneficial way.

DEVELOPING A STORYTELLER'S VOICE WITH WORDLESS PICTURE BOOKS

With a strong foundation in viewing and discussing images, it is an easy segue to wordless picture books that help students tell stories across several pages into one cohesive narrative. It helps if they have the three-step strategy of (1) challenge, (2) struggle, (3) hope. Telling a story across many pages is sometimes daunting for young writers, but a foundation in wordless picture books helps. When we read wordless picture books, we become invested in finding out whether the characters we've followed across several pages have their redemption moment. We linger on the page and develop close reading skills and oftentimes look back to remind ourselves of important details. So many reading process skills are better learned first with wordless picture books where decoding doesn't break down comprehension. Instead, the images tell the story, freeing us to focus on the narrative arc and our own feelings about what's happening across the pages.

When we weave wordless picture books into our read-aloud routines, we model the risk-taking needed to tell a story when the words aren't there. You can also pause to have students make predictions about what's going to happen next. Many wordless picture books have surprises that we don't see coming. This helps students recognize the value of surprising the reader in stories they themselves can write or illustrate.

Caldecott-winning *Wolf in the Snow* by Matthew Cordell (2017) captivates every group of students I've met. It's a book meant to be pored over again and again. In the beginning we see a girl with her family in a wintry landscape before she heads off to school. On her way home a huge snowstorm blows in, and she gets lost along the way. At the same time, a wolf pup gets away from its pack, and the two characters meet. After much struggle, both characters find redemption thanks to the unexpected help of others. The visually stunning book has echoes of Little Red Riding Hood, but *Wolf in the Snow* deliberately counters the narrative of wolves as dangerous. Cordell subtly asks readers to question their own assumptions about stories with girls in red hoods and wolves, and instead offers us a story of compassion and unexpected tenderness. This, in turn, helps readers build a habit of questioning previous stories they've heard when presented with a new kind of story.

To boost their storytelling voices with wordless picture books, students can use transition words like *first*, *next*, *then*, and *finally* to talk across pages. They can use choral reading for any single words that appear in places. They can meet in small groups to act out a wordless picture book by inventing the dialogue. You may also want to incorporate new technologies into the storytelling process to capture your students' voices by using apps like Voice Memos, Shadow Puppet, or Show Me, which offer audio, and in some cases, visual possibilities for students' storytelling selves to be captured and shared in new ways.

Some of my favorite wordless picture books for early childhood and upper elementary are those that tell stories of friendship and trust such as *The Lion and the Mouse* by Jerry Pinkney (2009), *Flora and the Flamingo* by Molly Idle (2013), *Red Sled* by Lita Judge (2011), *The Snowman* by Raymond Briggs (1978), and *Good Night, Gorilla* by Peggy Rathmann (2000). You can support elementary school students to build more nuanced inferences about what is happening and why using wordless books like *The Red Book* by Barbara Lehman (2004), *Mirror* by Jeannie Baker (2010), *Journey* by Aaron Becker (2013), *Flotsam* by David Weisner (2006), and *Unspoken: A Story from the Underground Railroad* by Henry Cole (2012).

LIFE STORIES THAT INVITE HOPEFUL POSSIBILITIES

When we design for happiness, we invite students to realize that their life story is constantly under revision. Reading about the life stories of others invites hopeful possibilities for students to imagine and reimagine their futures. As a fourth-grade teacher, I taught a group of girls who were fascinated by the fight women engaged in for the right to vote after reading *Who Was Susan B. Anthony?* by Pam Pollack and Meg Belviso (2014). They decided to research other women and girls who stood up for equal rights. Their reading led them to write and perform a skit for their classmates and families in our annual learning showcase. They wanted to not only present about these incredible women but also to become them. Reading life stories models for us the kind of lives we want to lead.

We support students to imagine future possibilities for themselves when we read aloud a range of books about diverse life experiences, particularly stories that follow the challenge-struggle-hope narrative format. My favorite books to share with students are life stories about people that are not household names but probably should be. Like Clara Lemlich featured in Michelle Markel's (2013) *Brave Girl: Clara and the Shirtwaist Makers' Strike of 1909.* As a young immigrant girl, Clara lands in New York City "dirt poor, just five feet tall, and hardly speaks a word of English." Her father is unable to find work, but Clara does as a seamstress in a garment factory. Full of grit and determination, Clara recognizes the injustices of the garment industry on the workers and organizes the girls to strike in the winter of 1909. Thousands of young girls line the streets of New York in protest of the working conditions. Clara's story models for readers the power of not only Clara's voice but the collective action of all of the girls who joined her side.

What if our students don't see their dreams coming true? How do we teach students the determination needed to pursue the life they want to live? In the early 1800s only white actors were allowed to perform Shakespeare. This didn't stop Ira Frederick Aldridge, who was spellbound by Shakespeare's *Hamlet* when he saw it at the Park Theater in New York City. *Ira's Shakespeare Dream* (Armand 2015), tells the story of Ira as a young African American boy who was not deterred by the injustice in America—instead, he pursued his dream by crossing the Atlantic to become one of the most celebrated Shakespearean actors of his time in England and across Europe.

Likewise, when a state law in Missouri made an education for African American children illegal, Reverend John Berry Meachum relocated his school from the basement of a church to the waters of the Mississippi River, creating a steamboat school. In addition to Deborah Hopkinton's *Steamboat School: Inspired by a True Story* (2016), there are many other heartrending books that describe the ways communities have fought for equal schools: *Rain School* by James Mumford (2010), *Separate Is Never Equal: Sylvia Mendez and Her Family's Fight for Desegregation* by Duncan Tonatiuh (2014), *The First Step: How One Girl Put Segregation on Trial* by Susan Goodman (2016), and *Malala Yousafzai: Warrior with Words* by Karen Leggett Abouraya (2019).

When students have access to a range of diverse life stories, they build the habit of asking themselves the important questions: "Is this my story?" and "Just who will I be?" Another pathway to students asking themselves these critical life questions is to read books where children are heroes. We see children as heroes in classic works like *The Lion, The Witch and the Wardrobe* by C. S. Lewis (1950) where a family of brothers and sisters stand up against the injustice of the White Witch. When Mr. Tumnus needs help they do not go back to the lamppost and through the wardrobe. They band together with the animals that need their help and they resist. But not without struggle, particularly for Edmund whose story is one that many children can relate to. When we are tempted by fortune or fame, which path do we choose? And how do we right ourselves if we go astray?

But we also see children as heroes in Pam Muñoz Ryan's (2015) body of work, particularly the genre-bending novel *Echo*. Told as a three-part narrative across time, readers encounter three children who are positioned as unlikely heroes against a backdrop of turmoil. Friedrich is born with a facial deformity and has to escape Nazi Germany. Mike is an orphan who must protect his brother during the Great Depression. Ivy is a Mexican American girl placed in a disadvantaged, segregated school in California. As the title suggests, each character's story echoes the one that came before it, revealing stories of fear, loneliness, and human atrocity. Even more powerful, though, are the echoes of hope, joy, and beauty that reverberate throughout this book. The characters are seeking something we all want in life: "to be free, to be loved, and to belong somewhere."

Our life stories are constantly being written. Nothing is permanent. This can be challenging for students to realize. We see them change, but it's important that they have texts that help them envision and recognize changes in themselves. Life stories help create a pathway for students to envision something great for their lives, and characters and historical figures give students models for how to get there.

In the weekly after-school litclub I run, Dayana and Janet read together *Of Thee I Sing: A Letter to My Daughters* by Barack Obama (2010) and illustrated by Lauren Long. As the girls analyzed the pages, they took notes about the qualities of a life well lived that they thought Barack Obama was telling them to strive for through his tribute to thirteen groundbreaking Americans written in the form of a letter to his daughters. Dayana and Janet shared with me afterward that reading this book made them feel like President Obama had given them the examples of these lives to inspire them to do something amazing with theirs.

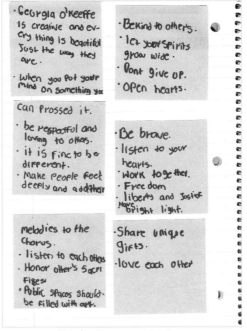

Reader Response Jottings

STORY SHARING AS A HAPPINESS ROUTINE

One of the greatest challenges I see many teachers facing is how to provide closure to lessons by building in time for students to share. It's usually the first thing to go when the schedule is tight and you have to get students to lunch, recess, or another important class. One way to establish story sharing as a routine in your classroom is to have a student job of "storyteller." With this job can come the responsibility of holding the teacher accountable to ensuring that sharing is a time built into every lesson, when possible, even if it means one voice is heard. Also with this job can come the option for the storyteller to share a story from their own life or from their imagination that falls outside of the curriculum. Stories like "My Name Story," "The First Time I _____ Story," "I Remember" stories, and "What if" stories can help get storytellers started (see the Appendix for more ideas). The storyteller could also share a story using other media and modes, like telling a story about a Legos or block structure they built, a story about a photograph they bring in to share, or a story about food that holds significance in their family. When our classrooms are full of stories, our students can recognize that we all care about things and people and we all struggle sometimes.

Happiness research also shows us that as humans we don't want to be fixed. We want to be acknowledged. Committing to classroom routines around stories can help students realize they are not alone, they are heard, and they are valued. The act of being listened to is ultimately an act of love. Well-told stories can help others or the storyteller see something in an entirely new way. Well-told stories create new connections. Well-told stories can change our minds and can even create a whole movement. The power of story is built into us. It's a part of our DNA. When we create routines around stories in our classrooms and build time for story sharing, we help students realize *why* stories matter.

A NOTE ON PERSONAL AND FICTIONAL NARRATIVES

> Alex
>
> December 13
>   A long time ago in a cookie galaxy far, far away.
>   GINGERBREAD WARS
> Episode II The Battle of Ginger-osis
> Cookie's too strong! I can't defeat
> him! Now, only master Obi-Wan can stop
> him Oh, please forgive me I am Anakin
> Dough-walker. As you may recall in
> the last episode, my son, Luke, was a
> cookie jedi and I played Evil Santa
> Claus. Well, that was just a preview. You
> say you don't know what's going on in the story? Well, I'll t-

> you. These days, there are people called
> gingerbread separatists These cookie are
> moving to far reaches of the galaxy.
> They've taken over the planet... well I
> don't really remember the name. But
> what ever the name was oh yeah!
> They've taken over the Ginger-osis.
> My master, Obi-Wan Ginger-obi, traveled
> to that planet and got captured by
> a robot called a cookie detai. My
> friend and I, Padmé Cookie, set out
> to look for him. Soon, we got captured

> Then, all three of us were sentenced
> to be crumbled. Soon we were chained
> and awaiting our final crumble
> If it hadn't been for Padmé, for
> she could get out of chains "Padmé
> ?!?! What are you doing !?!?!?" I
> shouted So, we escaped the clutches
> but soon thousands of battle cookie's
> and super battle cookies came out
> from a secret door and started shooting
> cookies But no sooner had they shooting
> when something happened

> The cookie jedi's came to the
> rescue! Soon, the evil cookie lord,
> Count Cookie entered. Then, Obi-Wan
> and I ignited our cookie sabers and
> began to fight In the end, we
> won the battle although Cookie
> had escaped After the battle,
> I felt like a cookie jedi because
> the cookie force fully flowed through
> me Suddenly, I saw something Another
> battle in my mind But that is another
> story The End.

Fiction Gingerbread Wars

Our life stories matter. The first time my son, Matthew, rode a bike, I told him he worked harder than any person I ever knew at anything. Matthew can use that experience to write a story about the reasons he wanted to ride a bike (rides to the candy store top the list), the struggles he had all summer, and, ultimately, the way he pushed and pulled his legs while I ran along beside him and how he didn't give up, even if he may have thrown his helmet a few times. I believe personal narratives have a place in our classrooms every year, if we are to come to know our students and all their dimensions, and if students are to come to know themselves and each other.

But I caution schools to recognize the need for fictional narratives in children's reading and writing lives. I sometimes visit schools where the single narrative unit for writers is personal narrative every year. I have even gone into classrooms for brief observations to see the same lesson being taught to kindergarteners all the way up to eighth graders using the language "Today, I will teach you." When students sit for the same lessons in the same genre year after year, we may capture some students who need repetition and deepening of ideas to strengthen their writing. But, we also have plenty of students who tune out because the repetition is simply too much. When students recognize that they have been a part of a lesson already, they get bored and tired. This is when you may see students talking to a neighbor when it's not the right time. Or you see some students wiggling in their seats. Or asking to go to the bathroom. When we oversaturate students with the same lessons on narrative, we create learning situations that lead to unhappiness rather than happiness. This is consistent with Marc Brackett's (2019) research out of the Yale Center for Emotional Intelligence, which surveyed thousands of students to gauge the emotional temperature of today's students. Brackett found that students routinely responded with "bored" or "tired," which led his team to create the signature RULER program that gives students an outlet for recognizing, understanding, labeling, expressing, and regulating emotion. While students can learn to gauge and redirect their emotions, our curricular choices play a significant role in constructing the experiences students have in school.

So, what's the solution? We want students to have foundational skills in how narratives work and why they are important. Whether students are writing from their lives or from their imaginations, it's the same skill set. But I urge literacy leaders and classroom teachers to take a look at their school to see whether personal narrative is the driver every year or whether imaginative narratives can help students apply similar lessons about stories in a new way. Does it matter whether students write personal narratives or fiction, or can students be trusted to choose which genre fits the ideas they have? Does it matter if they are telling a true story, or does it matter more that they apply craft strategies and have a story worth telling? When we create flexibility for students in the kinds of stories they write and how they communicate them, we intentionally design for student happiness alongside student learning.

DESIGN FOR STORY

- Teach the secrets of stories using a three-part structure: challenge-struggle-hope.
- Create a "Stories Are Everywhere" interactive board that encourages students to jot down the seed of a story based on something they see or hear.
- Use quickwrites to get students talking, writing, drawing, and sharing:

A time I was really happy (sad, annoyed, elated, surprised, proud, confused)

A time I was upset by someone else

A time I lost something (maybe it was found)

A time I wished something were different

A time I was changed

A memory I have is _____ .

The first time I _____ .

The last time I _____ .

What if . . .?

- Gradually teach craft techniques to strengthen students' stories.
- Incorporate image reading as a storytelling routine.
- Immerse students in wordless picture books to grow their storyteller's voices.
- Investigate life stories through powerful, lesser known stories about people that made a difference in the lives of others.
- Create a story-sharing routine as part of your day's closure.
- Encourage students to choose whether they write a personal narrative or imaginative one.

Chapter 7

Discovery

It is a happiness to wonder;
it is a happiness to dream.

—Edgar Allen Poe

CLASSROOM STORY: EXPLORING BOOKS

In Stacy's first-grade class, children are exploring different kinds of books and different kinds of stories. The children are accustomed to sorting books according to whether they are fiction or nonfiction from when they were in kindergarten, but this is the first time they are thinking deeply about the different kinds of stories they see in books. Stacy has spread books out across the classroom rug. She has selected stories that she knows her students gravitate toward with excitement year after year: Mo Willems' Elephant and Piggie books, popular picture books like Drew Daywalt (2013) *The Day the Crayons Quit*, and lots of Mac Barnett (2017, 2018) and Jon Klassen (2012) books like *Triangle*, *Square*, and *This Is Not My Hat*. While children pore over the books, they are encouraged to share their thinking. Stacy wants them to find the language that works for them to explain what they see before she gives them the academic language that can overcomplicate their thinking.

The goal of this exploration was to start an inquiry together into different kinds of stories that could keep growing throughout the year. In my role in her classroom, I gently encouraged children to keep exploring, noticing, wondering, and sharing. Children shared noticings like: "I see Square in both of these books" (explaining how the character Square is in both *Triangle* and *Square*) and "Ooh, ooh, I think these two are by the same author" (holding up Cynthia Rylant's *Henry and Mudge The First Book* (1996) and *Poppleton* (1996)). At the end of this exploration session, the children helped me create a class chart on different types of stories that could serve as a running list throughout the year. The children created categories like: books that make us laugh (*Should I Share My Ice Cream?* (Willems 2011), *Fox+Chick: The Party and Other Stories* (Ruzzier 2018), *Triangle* and *Square*), books that have clever drawings (*The Day the Crayons Quit* [Daywalt 2013]), books that include photos and illustrations (*Knuffle Bunny: A Cautionary Tale* [Willems 2004]), books we want to read with a friend (*Henry and Mudge: The First Book* [Rylant

1996]), and books that make us look at each page a long time (*The Red Book* [Lehman 2004]). We were designing instruction to maximize the feelings associated with discovery: awe, wonder, revelation, and fascination. We can make discovery and wonder a key part of workshop instruction when we hold back from leading with our ideas and instead give more space for children to explore their own thinking first. In the traditional gradual release of responsibility model of "I do—we do—you do," inquiry can get lost. But when we intentionally build in genuine inquiry and exploration, children come first and we flip the model to "you do—we do—I do."

After the book exploration, we read aloud Mac Barnett (2017) *Triangle* to continue our focus on discovery and wonder. Rather than didactically ending the book with a lesson or moral, Barnett instead ends with the question, "But do you believe him really?" Intentionally ending the book with a question invites young readers to form the habit of wondering at the end of stories. They use this same technique with their next book, *Square*, by ending the story with a similar question—"But was he really?" The questions position readers to wonder if the characters really say what they mean and mean what they say. These are questions readers can ask themselves across books as characters get more complex, more dynamic, and more lifelike. What Barnett and Klassen's books do brilliantly is let young readers in on an important secret—great stories leave us with questions, and it's okay that we may never really know the answer. Anytime you want to infuse discovery and wonder into your lessons, turn to Barnett (2012) and Klassen as models by using other books of theirs like *Extra Yarn* and Klassen's (2011, 2012, 2016) hatty oeuvre *I Want My Hat Back*, *This Is Not My Hat*, and *We Found a Hat*.

In Stacy's class in the weeks to come, the children embraced the spirit of discovery and wonder. Stacy reminded them before each independent reading time that one of the great gifts we get from reading is the invitation to discover something new and to keep wondering long after we close the book. When I returned several weeks later, the children shared with me more of their wonderings about stories and the kinds of questions they were now asking at the end of books. *Elephant and Piggie's Should I Share My Ice Cream?* by Mo Willems (2011) helped one boy ask: "What would I do?" and "What makes someone a good friend?" Likewise, when another student finished exploring Seymour Simon's *Earth* (2003), he asked: "What do we still not know about our planet?" Inquiry was now embedded into reading workshop, and there was no turning back. The children had come to learn that we deepen our reading lives by asking questions.

Some of the goals of an inquiry-driven classroom are to help students connect, extend, and challenge. Inquiry happens every time we stand at a bookshelf and wonder what to read next. Inquiry happens when we stare at the blank page and wonder how to begin. Inquiry happens when you ask someone a question that you don't already know the answer to. Having a stance toward inquiry is central to literacy learning. Brooks (2004) reminds us that "All of us want to know how the world works; why a piece of music is beautiful to one person and cacophonous to another, how engines are able to make cars move, why green leaves turn brown and helium balloons stay aloft, or how new languages develop. Living means perpetually searching for meaning" (12). Literacy instruction offers teachers a time to keep that search for meaning alive.

RESEARCH SAYS: SEEING THE WORLD WITH WONDER AND AWE

Think about a time when you looked up at the stars on a clear night, or saw a harvest moon on your drive home from work, or noticed the changes in leaf color from one day to the next. Awe is the sense of wonder we experience when we are in the presence of something that allows us to pause and take notice of the world around us in a new way. Although we often pay attention to this feeling the most when we are in nature, we also experience this sense of awe and the wonder associated with it when we look at a painting or listen to music or watch someone do something that amazes us. My two children experience a sense of awe when they watch People Are Awesome on YouTube.

Researchers in the field of social psychology (Keltner and Haidt 2003) found that experiencing a sense of awe does more than give us pause and appreciation for the world and our place in it. They found that when we experience a sense of awe, it also promotes altruism, loving kindness, and magnanimous behavior. In each of their experiments, they found that when people experienced a sense of awe they became less self-important and showed prosocial behaviors. When we experience awe, we are more likely to become more invested in the greater good and to help others. All of which are directly connected to building a life of sustainable happiness.

Literacy learning is full of possibilities for building a sense of awe and wonder in students whether you get students outside to look closely at the world around them and to tap into their senses or whether you project the image of a painting that has mystified people for decades or even centuries and give students space or strategies to say what they see. Or you play a song that takes your students to another place in their imagination before they begin their own writing. Or you invite students to book browse a variety of picture books on the classroom rug, so they can discover something new.

Creating experiences where children discover more about themselves and the world helps students realize that their questions are worth asking. When you know your questions are valued, your curiosity grows, and so does your confidence. Researchers continue to make new discoveries for how to live a more joyful life, but one key finding is that curious people—those who are constantly asking questions and looking for new possibilities—tend to enjoy higher levels of positive emotions, lower levels of anxiety, more satisfaction with life, and greater psychological well-being.

SELF-DISCOVERY: WHAT FEELS GOOD? WHAT FEELS HARD?

One of the simplest techniques to help children to ask questions about themselves while asking questions of texts is to ground conferring practices around two key questions: What feels good in your reading/writing today, and what feels hard? I've found that when these questions routinely drive conferring it helps students to start internalizing these questions for themselves. To feel successful as our reading and writing lives get more complex requires the self-knowledge that comes from the long-term benefits of constantly learning more about ourselves.

When visiting a primary school in London for children ages three to ten, I had an opportunity to spend time in classrooms driven by inquiry as the heart of all instruction. In year five (fourth grade) students were working in small groups to strengthen their understanding of how to use punctuation when writing dialogue by writing their own final scenes to the folktale Baba Yaga. As children worked on their scenes, I approached students with the question, "What feels good in your writing today?" I was a stranger to them, but the question allowed them to open up and share. One boy replied that it felt good to know the rules for punctuation within dialogue because he was surprised that he didn't know them before. Another boy replied that it felt good to be at this stage in his writing where he was in command of the conventions and could devote his brain power to his ideas. A girl sitting in the corner spoke about how it felt good to use words other than *said*, thanks to practice she did with classmates the day before. Every student I approached had a thoughtful, personal response. What struck me most about all of the children's responses was that they seemed to sit up a little straighter when they responded and that they felt confident in what they were saying.

Interestingly, in this classroom children are routinely instructed in small groups with whole-class instruction minimized. With small-group instruction as the default, children are conditioned to reflect on the purpose of their learning since each lesson is targeted for students to continuously discover something new. Small-group instruction is also a great time to ask students what feels good or what feels hard in their reading and writing either at the start of small-group lessons or as closure.

CHOOSE, ACT, REFLECT

Some schools I visit are driven by exploration, discovery, and wonder. The hallway and classroom walls are lined with children's attempts to make meaning by thinking, feeling, and, most importantly, acting. If as literacy learners children are positioned to continuously reflect on themselves and their place in the world, we deepen the impact of that work by expecting children to take action in some way. Rather than leave this open ended, we can design tangible ways for students to take action by extending children's reading and writing lives to make the world a better place.

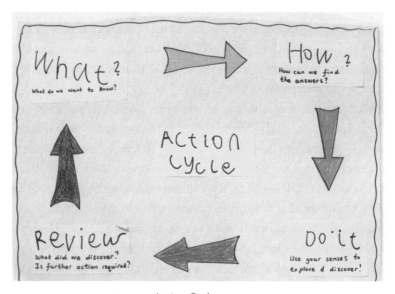

Action Cycle

When children are positioned as ambassadors of their learning, they feel trusted to try, ask for help when they need it, and extend their learning beyond the page and into the world. One way to encourage them to see themselves as ambassadors of their own learning is to engage them in action cycles that incorporate a chance to choose, act, and reflect. This cycle fosters in students the confidence to make decisions and see what happens. This habit of making choices, taking action, and reflecting fosters a deep sense of discovery needed for the roots of sustainable happiness to take hold in childhood.

Encouraging students to reflect about how they want to take action can begin by supporting them to consider what they hope to accomplish and whether they want to:

- build something to help others
- design a solution
- help prevent a problem
- change their own behavior and choices
- inspire others to change
- inform others.

Based on what they want to accomplish, they can be supported to consider what actions they can take to make those goals a reality. Students can then be supported to think and write about how they did take action and what happened as a result.

Inquiry Cycle

Going one step further, I have partnered with schools to develop capstone projects, particularly at the middle school level where students are supported to engage in an inquiry cycle around a topic they feel passionate about, that they want to take action toward, and that they want to persuade others to care about. Students have created capstone projects on a myriad of topics ranging from crocheting for a cause to raising awareness about the continuous melting of the polar ice caps. Creating curriculum that is inquiry-driven requires rethinking what we hope students will gain as a result of their projects. Overwhelmingly, teachers report that the leadership skills their students gain are just as valuable as the academic skills they gain, if not more so. Growing their flexibility, reflection, persistence, and risk-taking capacities are often cited as the greatest gains from the choose, act, reflect process students engage in through their capstone projects.

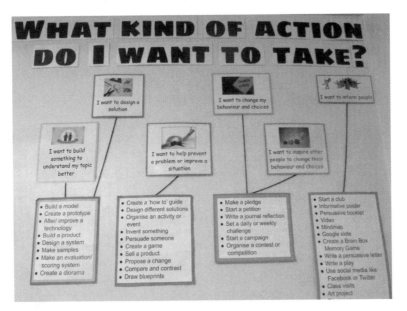

Kinds of Actions to Take

WHAT'S WORTH ASKING?

Yet, some students have difficulty knowing what's worth asking. It takes practice to ask a worthwhile question. As students are encouraged to discover things about themselves and the world through a deliberate process of action and reflection, students become more confident posing questions and looking for solutions. In an inquiry-driven classroom, teachers deliberately encourage and celebrate questions and help students learn about how to ask different kinds of questions. In a classroom devoted to discovery and action, question posing becomes more natural. By asking questions routinely, students are able to create new categories of thought and experience. Questioning activates thinking. The stronger the questions, the more empowered students are as learners to plan, problem solve, self-assess, and create. Students begin to think about what's worth inquiring about and are able to pose open-ended questions like:

- What am I learning?
- What connections am I making?
- What do I understand?
- When do I do my best thinking?
- Who can help me strengthen my ideas?
- What does this remind me of?
- What am I noticing?
- What am I wondering?
- What can help me remember what I've learned?

They are also able to pose and consider literacy-specific questions like:

- What makes a great story?
- Is this story also my story? How?
- What makes a great poem?
- What are different kinds of stories?
- What connections do I have to this story? What disconnections?
- What advice could I give to this character? Author?
- What new information am I gaining?
- Do I agree with this author? Why or why not?
- What's different? What's the same?

When our literacy instruction is guided by overarching worthwhile questions, students are able to discern what kinds of questions are worth asking. There are also literacy practices we can link questioning to. One way of encouraging students to see the link between question posing and book choice is to label nonfiction book baskets with question words: *Who? What? Where? When? How? Why?* This simple technique models for students the expectation that books will inherently spark the inquirer in them and that the reading process activates the question-posing part of ourselves. Making question words public also helps students get a running start in asking their own questions.

Ultimately posing questions inspires in students the sense that solving some of the world's most complicated issues will come by asking the right questions. Research on brainstorming from Hal Gregerson (2018), Executive Director of the MIT Leadership Center, now shows us that the most generative brainstorming sessions come from an initial period of simply asking any questions that come to mind. Gregerson argues that from a young age we are positioned to give answers, not to arrive at solutions by asking questions. Yet, it is precisely asking questions that leads to breakthrough approaches. We can apply Gregerson's research in our classrooms, by shifting brainstorming to a process focused on questions rather than ideas. By first asking any and all questions for a set period of time, students are then able to look at their collaborative list of questions and discern which are the questions really worthy of pursuing.

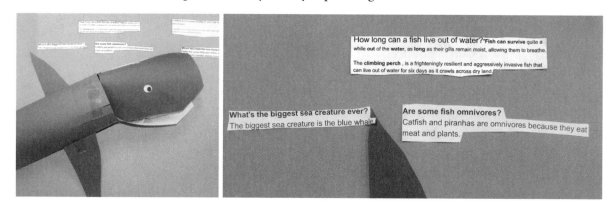

All About Sharks Questions and Answers

The more students build a habit of asking questions, the more they will challenge their own deeply held assumptions and come up with new and innovative ways of looking at problems.

CHARACTERS MODEL QUESTIONING

Many of us will spend our lifetimes searching for the answer to happiness. But, perhaps we need to be learning to ask questions instead of searching for answers. Instead of believing that happiness is given or taken, we can learn to ask, "How can I choose happiness today?" Instead of saying, "I'm stuck," we can learn to ask, "What else can I try?" Instead of feeling powerless, we can learn to ask, "How can I feel strong right now?" This shift to asking questions helps children move past apathy and toward action.

Over the past few years, children's literature has offered readers a plethora of characters that model the power of questioning. In *The Antlered Ship* by Dashka Slater (2017), a philosophical fox named Marco is suddenly filled with quixotic questions when a mysterious antlered ship arrives near his home: "Why do some songs make you happy and others make you sad? Why don't trees ever talk? How deep does the sun go when it sinks into the sea?" In the end, he finds satisfaction not from finding the answer to these questions but by asking a new and even more important question: "What's the best way to find a friend you can talk to?" The brilliance of Marco is that he is like many of our students. He wonders aloud about lots of things that interest him. His questions matter. But his questions also evolve. Learning to ask questions that help us choose happiness can be hard. Luckily, characters like Marco model the meandering path our questions take us in life as well as the way to ask questions that help us find inner meaning and meaning beyond ourselves.

In *Why Am I Me?* Paige Britt (2017) makes it clear from the title that life is full of big and important questions that do not have easy answers. The main character asks, "Why am I me . . . and not you? Why are you, you . . . and not me?" These seemingly simple yet profoundly philosophical questions are ones children are already asking as they make sense of themselves and the world around them. When paired with Kobi Yamada's (2014, 2016, 2018) trio of books *What Do You Do with an Idea?, What Do You Do with a Problem?,* and *What Do You Do with a Chance?,* you can start to build a text set devoted to the power of wondering about life's big questions including questions of personal identity.

Sometimes the questions children ask are less philosophical but no less important to the children asking them. Dan Santat's (2016) *Are We There Yet?* takes the childhood refrain heard on car trips and invites readers to imagine what happens when your brain becomes too bored. As with his Caldecott-winning *The Adventures of Beekle: The Unimaginary Friend* (2014), Santat surprises readers, this time with an allegory on the gift of boredom to help us savor the present. By literally turning a boring situation upside down, readers are invited to turn the book upside down to see where the protagonist's boredom takes him. The message is subtle, and Santat allows readers to wonder about where boredom can take them.

The world of children's literature is full of characters that offer models of the power of questioning, but even books themselves can serve as models. In *This Is Not a Book* written and illustrated by Jean Jullien (2016), readers are positioned to wonder when a book is not a book. This nearly wordless picture book cleverly transforms the familiar board book into something else altogether. Readers are invited to play with the book's position like flapping pages to make a butterfly. These interactions encourage shifts in perspective but also new kinds of questions.

These books show us that inquiry-driven classrooms can also be story-driven classrooms. Children's literature will keep evolving, offering readers new ways to interact, shift perspectives, and ask a range of questions. Advances in children's literature have made discovery a primary reason for reading. The more we incorporate these works of children's literature into our read-alouds and minilessons and as mentor texts for students as writers, the more our students will connect literacy learning with the feelings of discovery and wonder.

THE NATURAL WORLD

It's no secret that time in nature makes our minds and our bodies healthier and happier. A growing body of research is finding that just about any kind of green space can make you happier and can boost your mental health. Time spent in nature has been found to help reduce anxiety and stress and increases our attention capacity, creativity, and ability to connect with other people. Science is finally catching up to what writers like Thoreau, John Muir, and Terry Tempest Williams have been discussing for the last 100 years. Yet, children are spending more time indoors and online. Findings on how nature improves our brains and our happiness bring added legitimacy for preserving and using natural spaces but also for teachers to use the natural world as a resource for all kinds of learning experiences including literacy learning.

If our classrooms are devoted to discovery and wonder as an instructional pillar in designing for happiness, we can consider the natural world another classroom or bring the natural world into the classroom. When children have the time to look, notice, wonder, record, draw, and write about what they see in nature, their literacy skills and their happiness are boosted. As a fourth-grade teacher in New York City, my class was fortunate to tend a small, urban garden plot for the school. Every Friday in the fall and spring, we took our clipboards and colored pencils along with our trowels and rakes.

Everyone contributed. Everyone jotted and sketched. Everyone found quiet corners and had time to think. The time we spent in the garden produced tomato plants and flowers. It also produced poetry, artwork, and stories. More importantly, it helped my students connect, extend, and challenge themselves in new ways. How can I help the garden today? Where is the best spot for me to reflect and write? What do I notice? What do I wonder?

Children's literature is blessed with books that help us bring nature indoors. *Sidewalk Flowers* by JonArno Lawson (2015) is a nearly wordless picture book about a child's noticing of the flowers that grow inside the sidewalk cracks while out for a neighborhood walk with her father. Her distracted father pays her little attention, but the girl finds her own happiness thanks to nature's reminder that beauty can be found in unlikely places. Similarly, in *Tiny, Perfect Things* by M.H. Clark (2018), a girl is out for a walk with her grandfather. A seemingly ordinary day turns into a grand adventure where nature provides the catalyst for wonder. Kate Messner's (2011, 2015, 2017) books *Over and Under the Snow*, *Up in the Garden and Down in the Dirt*, *Over and Under the Pond*, and are some of my favorites for bringing nature into the classroom through literature. Through sparse, poetic text, Messner invites readers into the discovery process of the natural world along with the characters. It's like we, too, are gliding through the woodland on skis, peering into a pond from a canoe, and digging in the dirt. Books like Philip Stead's (2016) *Ideas Are All Around* remind us that an antidote for writer's block is right in front of you. As the narrator and his trusty dog, Wednesday, stroll the neighborhood, they encounter objects, animals, and people. His walk around the neighborhood leads to a "walk around the page."

To invite students to notice and wonder throughout the year, consider introducing window spots at the beginning of the year that give students special places to notice and wonder when they need to. Gather paper towel rolls as lookout tools to help student zoom in on small things they see by looking out the window. Incorporate sketching, photographing, and jotting about nature as a spark for writing across genres. If heading on a neighborhood walk is possible, ask permission, and make it happen. Notice nature as well as graffiti, billboards, and signs. Take a sound walk inside or outside where students get to listen more than look, jotting down the sounds they hear as inspiration for further writing. Take a lookup walk where students are encouraged to look up to notice what they see by changing the direction of their focus. Clouds, buildings, birds, planes, and the sun can all serve as inspiration.

Like Stead, take a walk around the neighborhood and then a walk around the page. If it's not possible, create a simple sensory bin for students to notice and wonder. Fill it with snow, dirt, leaves, sticks, acorns, anything you can find that will spark opportunities for students to connect with nature and continuously discover something new. Encourage slowing down. Encourage students to get to know nature in their own home neighborhoods. The sky, the sun, and the moon always anchor us as humans wherever we live. This gives us a natural pathway for supporting students to create their own sky journals or moon journals through writing, drawing, or photography to link literacy learning with a sense of awe and wonder in the most fundamental ways.

THE GIFT OF TIME

Learning from leaders of innovation like Google and Amazon, schools have started strategically designing for students to have the gift of time to engage in the thought processes needed for discovery and wonder to take flight. Schools call it many things:

- I-Time
- Discovery Time
- Genius Hour
- Innovation Day
- Passion Projects

What they have in common is that students can count on scheduled times in the day or week to ask their own questions, to pursue their own answers, and to share their findings in ways that allow them to express themselves in meaningful ways. In many ways Discovery Time has its origins in John Dewey's educational philosophies rooted in problem solving and learning by doing. Sometimes that means something in the schedule has to shift for this gift of time to be possible for all students. Yes, independent reading time matters. Independent writing time matters. Explicit instruction time matters. Foundational skills time matters. True discovery time matters as well.

If we frame what counts in our classrooms, then time is the currency of education. Consider with colleagues how to incorporate a scheduled block of time for students to ask their own questions, to research their own answers using a variety of techniques, and to share what they've found with an audience. Justifying open-ended discovery time can be hard in our era of accountability. Luckily, A. J. Juliani (2014) has collected research behind the Genius Hour concept and student choice. Her book *Inquiry and Innovation in the Classroom* provides guidelines for how to prepare your class and support student projects at the elementary or secondary levels. We cannot explicitly teach innovation, but we can provide the gift of time for students to ask questions that interest them, and we can support them to use their strengths as literacy learners to read and write in pursuit of discovery and to share their findings.

Some questions and ideas students asked in my fourth-grade class during Discovery Time were things like:

- Where can I look for inspiration to write and record my own song?
- How can I make my own website?
- How can I make a cake for my mom without her knowing?
- I want to find out more about designing buildings.
- I want to find out more about designing video games.

Wonder Wall

Discovery Time, much like book choice, is not anything goes. As with book choice, we can begin the process of introducing Discovery Time by modeling our own process of discovery in our own lives. We can then engage the class in shared Discovery Time by choosing a class topic that the class decides upon with students in Inquiry Teams dedicated to different kinds of research like online searching, book searches, and interviews with community members. Yes, you can link this shared Discovery Time to science and social studies topics, but you can also trust the process and the gift of time by allowing students to select a topic that fills them with burning questions: How do rollercoasters work? Why are whales in Alaska in danger? How can we help our family members to get along? The class is likely to draw from their own experiences, along with their wishes, hopes, and dreams. Giving students time to explore their biggest and most important life questions will always be time well spent.

We can also scaffold the process by asking our own questions of students to help ignite and propel wonder on a regular basis:

- Wouldn't it be amazing if . . . ?

- What if . . . ?

- Have you ever . . . ?

- What does that make you wonder?

- What makes you say that?

- How is your thinking changing?

- What an interesting question . . . I wonder where you might take that idea?

- Can you give an example of that?

- What connection can you make?

- What do you think helped you?

- What would someone who disagreed with you say? How would you respond to that?

- Do you think that is always true?

- How will you know if you've met your goal?

We can also use prompts that allow students to ponder and decide for themselves like:

- Tell me more about . . .

- Maybe . . .

- Possibly . . .

- Might . . .

- Could . . .

- Keep your eyes and ears open for . . .

If open-ended inquiry is too complex to enact, consider other models that open up student choice in their learning such as project-based learning, which utilizes structured inquiry or guided inquiry. In structured inquiry students follow the lead of the teacher as the class engages in one inquiry together. In guided inquiry teachers choose the topics or questions, and students design products or solutions, often in inquiry teams. Research led by literacy experts Nell Duke and Anne-Lise Halvorsen (2017) through the University of Michigan and Michigan State University found that after a year of project-based learning, students whose teachers were randomly assigned to instruct through projects posted higher scores on a social studies test created by the researchers than schoolmates who were instructed as usual.

Although Discovery Time is best scheduled in a way that all students can participate, we also want to communicate to students through our language choices and actions that discovery and wonder are lifelong ways of being that can lead to happier lives. Students won't need convincing.

Finally, the wonders of the Internet have given us as educators resources that allow discovery and wonder to flourish. Some of my favorite are:

Wonderopolis wonderopolis.com	Explore wonder prompts and add a wondering of your own. Follow Student Wonder.
Mix mix.com	Curate a collection of wonderings. Discover your next favorite thing by going deeper into topics and then sharing what you find with others.
Literacy Shed literacyshed.com	Explore with students "sheds" like Adventure Shed, Fantasy Shed, and Inventors Shed full of short films and animations that spark awe and wonder.
Curiosity curiosity.com	Web page is grouped by Amazing Places, Brilliant Products, Food and Culture, Mind and Body, Personal Growth, Science and Technology, and more. Content is question driven and serves as models for students to ask a range of questions about a range of topics.
National Geographic for Kids kids.nationalgeographic.com	This interactive site has videos, articles, and images designed to inspire the explorer in every child.

DESIGN FOR DISCOVERY

- Invite students to discover new things about books by sorting books in new ways.
- Engage students in inquiry cycles by having them follow a process of choose, act, reflect.
- Support students to refine their questions by considering "What's worth asking?"
- Model with your own questions, or use some of the ones provided in this chapter.
- Support students to notice the ways that characters model questioning.
- Tap into the natural world wherever you are as a source of awe and wonder.
- Schedule discovery time as a way to support students to ask questions, make choices, and take action.

Chapter 8

Movement

> One of the greatest mistakes of our day is to think of movement by itself, as something apart from the higher functions . . . Watching a child makes it obvious that the development of his mind comes about through his movements.
>
> —Maria Montessori

CLASSROOM STORY: BECOMING THE CHARACTERS

While listening to *Harry Potter and the Sorcerer's Stone* by J. K. Rowling (2016) enchantingly illustrated by Jim Kay, students in Joe's third-grade class lean forward, eager to hear Harry's latest triumphs and tribulations. They also wait eagerly for the next illustration by Jim Kay, which will transport them to Harry's world. The classroom feels electric with anticipation. Joe's voice adds to the power of the fantasy, carrying his students from their classroom and into the imagined world that Rowling created. During my visit, the class is at the part where Harry walks into a pub in Diagon Alley and finds himself shaking hands with everyone. Joe reads with a different voice for each character that greets Harry. When he comes to the part where Harry shakes hands with each of the pub's patrons again and again, Joe encourages his class to turn and shake hands with one another. All of the students are now smiling, shaking hands with each other, and the meaning of this unexpected moment for Harry becomes more meaningful and relevant. This interaction wasn't by accident. Joe was intentional in the selection of this passage as an opportunity for intentional movement, or purposeful, planned movement.

Joe knows that intentionally providing opportunities for his students to tap into their bodies helps strengthen their connections to the stories he reads aloud, furthers their word knowledge, and gives them a spark of joy. He also knows the research on how important our connections to our own bodies are to feelings of power and possibility. Amy Cuddy's (2015) research detailed in her bestselling book *Presence: Bringing Your Boldest Self to Your Biggest Challenges* shows that our bodies don't just carry us where we want to go: they can also help carry us to who we want to be. Where our bodies lead, our minds and emotions will follow. She explains that "the body moves, speaks, responds, breathes, lives because of the brain. The body and brain are part of a single, integrated, complicated, beautiful system" (73).

Joe builds intentional movement into his read-alouds to help his students connect to the characters, their actions, and their emotions. He also takes time to teach his students about how the way we carry ourselves from moment to moment blazes the trail our lives take. If he can help his students understand that the way you carry yourself is a source of personal power, they can make choices that will give them greater happiness. Connecting with our bodies gives us the kind of power that is key to presence. As Cuddy explains, "It's the key that allows you to unlock yourself—your abilities, your creativity, your courage, and even your generosity" (198). When we feel more present both physically and mentally, we are better able to share the skills and talents we have. We become more resilient and open. Being more present doesn't change who you are, but it allows you to *be* who you are.

Think about when you feel at your most powerful. When we feel powerful, we stretch out. We lift our chins and pull our shoulders back. We spread our feet apart, and we raise our arms like a gymnast at the end of a vault routine or a runner breaking through the ribbon at the finish line. As a child, my dad always had us pose with our arms up in the air when he was taking photos of us. He instinctively knew that this was a power pose and that if he directed us to try it for the photo, maybe we'd feel more powerful. My dad wanted us to

Power Pose

carry ourselves with pride and to embody confidence and courage as a source of personal power. It works. Find a quiet, private space and try it. Lift your arms up in the air like you just landed a vault dismount at the Olympics. Or stretch your arms out wide like you just crossed the finish line at the Boston Marathon. Find images online of runners and gymnasts in "power poses," and have your students try their favorite power poses, too. Build in classroom routines, particularly at the start of literacy lessons or independent reading or writing, where students can take a moment to show their favorite power pose. They'll be more ready to read and write with purpose and power, and you will see more smiles on their faces. Their power pose may be a dab or the latest craze, the pickle, and that's fine. They need to own their power pose to tap into it when they need it most.

Planning for intentional movement as a part of literacy learning can be achieved in many different ways. One simple method is to preview read-alouds like Joe to select key moments where students can quickly enact a physical connection to the text. Authors who use powerful verbs make this planning even easier for us as teachers. One of my favorite ways to incorporate movement is when reading aloud from *Alexander and the Terrible, Horrible, No Good, Very Bad Day* by Judith Viorst (1972). She uses words like *scrunched* and *smooshed* to describe Alexander in the car with his carpool. As each turn of events leaves Alexander more despondent, Viorst uses language that describes what Alexander did and how he was feeling. Authors use language to invite us to imagine the scenes their words describe. When we use children's literature that sparks our imaginations and that is full of rich, vivid language, we can invite our students to use their bodies to quickly express meaning. When we do so, we tap into a powerful pathway for memory for students to hold onto what they have heard or read now and for future use by strengthening the schema students have as they build word associations.

RESEARCH SAYS: LEVERAGING THE BODY-MIND CONNECTION

Children especially are built to move, watch things move, and make things move. Children are inherently motivated by being connected in some way to movement. The word *motivation* is actually from the medieval Latin *motivus*, which literally means "moving" or "motion." Research from across fields helps show us why movement is so essential for learning.

We can incorporate intentional movement into word study or vocabulary or academic language study. In the article "Move It or Lose It" in *Educational Leadership*, authors Linnea Lyding, Debby Zambo, and Cory Cooper Hansen (2014) describe the ways they used purposeful, planned movement to help students remember and apply terms associated with the water cycle. They define *purposeful, planned movement* as a range of strategies—from short activity breaks, to gestures that create mental imagery for key concepts, to more far-ranging activities like role playing and dramatic interpretations. Their work was spurred on by the classroom realities of students sitting for longer periods of time for more direct instruction by teachers across subjects. Building intentional movement into lessons helps meet students' physical, emotional, and cognitive needs. It also gives them tools for sustained happiness that they can apply in their own lives.

In addition to increasing meaning, purpose, and joy, designing for intentional movement can help children from all backgrounds in literacy and in life. Children who come from a history of trauma often have a "fight-flight-or-freeze" response to threatening situations. When I was visiting a kindergarten classroom where the majority of children came from some form of childhood trauma, several children (all happened to be boys) were exhibiting fight-flight-or-freeze responses to the overload they were experiencing during explicit phonics instruction. Their fists were balled. Their breathing was rapid and shallow. When children's brains are flooded with new information, this can trigger fight-flight-or-freeze responses. You may see them disrupting instruction, running out of the classroom, hiding behind classroom structures, or using their bodies in dangerous ways. Their brains and their bodies are connected, and their bodies are letting us know that what is being asked is simply too much.

The National Survey of Children's Health (Data Resource Center for Child and Adolescent Health 2016) has found that in the United States alone over thirty-five million children have experienced one or more types of trauma. Almost half of the nation's children have at least one or more types of serious childhood trauma. Brain science has found that the amygdala and the hippocampus are two brain structures involved in fear and traumatic stress. The amygdala detects whether a stimulus (person or event) is threatening, and the hippocampus, the center of short-term memory, links the fear response to the context in which the threatening stimulus or event occurred. These two brain structures also play an important role in the release of stress hormones such as cortisol and adrenaline influencing the capacity of the prefrontal cortex for regulating thought, emotions, and actions, as well as keeping information readily accessible during active learning. Fight-flight-or-freeze responses are self-protection. They are natural and understandable. But they erode learning. Instead of waiting for students to use their bodies to tell us when their learning expectations are too much, we can incorporate intentional movement in positive ways by design.

Some ways to counter the fight-flight-or-freeze instincts some children have to new learning directly incorporates intentional movement. Doing something physical and positive helps reorient the body and the mind in a positive way. Our bodies speak to us. They tell us how and what to feel and even think. Jump it out. Clap it out. March it out. These are all things we can have students intentionally do at the start of literacy lessons or at appropriate moments in read-alouds to help students tap into their bodies in a positive way. In her book *Activate: Deep Learning Through Movement, Talk, and Flexible Classrooms,* Katherine Mills Hernandez (2018) deeply explores the science behind how movement supports learning but she also shares strategies for incorporating movement in meaningful ways through a repertoire of "moves" including:

- **Walkie Talkie:** two-minute walk-and-talk break midway through a long lesson
- **Move It!:** twenty jumping jacks followed by careful stretches and deep breaths in the middle of a lesson
- **Scavengers, Engage:** find objects around the room that are part of the demonstration of a lesson
- **The Outfield:** take your lesson outdoors
- **Zone Shift:** moving the class to a different part of the room for the second half of a lesson
- **Game Time:** a quick partner game like rock, paper, scissors before or in the middle of a lesson
- **Pop Quiz Catch:** incorporate a small ball or soft object to have students answer questions
- **Stand, If You Please:** offer students the chance to stand when they need to.

We can also help students practice calm biology by incorporating breathing exercises that help students recognize the ways their bodies are connected to their brains. Turn off or lower the lights. Emphasize quiet stillness. Then have students breathe and exhale slowly and deeply through the nose. Have students place one hand on their belly and one hand on their rib cage, so they can feel the power of their breathing. Call it "joy breathing." Just one minute of joy breathing as a ritual can help recenter children's bodies so that their minds are ready for learning. This is simple to incorporate to your classroom literacy routine by intentionally building one minute of intentional breathing before students transition from the read-aloud to independent reading or from the classroom rug back to their seats.

One of the most important things to be aware of when designing for intentional movement is whether you want students to turn it up or calm it down. When we build in active intentional movements like clapping, stomping, or marching, students' bodies will be heightened as will their minds. This is best when it is a quick burst such as during a read-aloud or before students are heading off to do something active like independent or collaborative writing. If you incorporate very active intentional movement and then expect students to silently read, it may backfire. However, if you incorporate intentional, slow breathing before independent reading, it may work smoothly. When we leverage the mind-body connection and respond to the natural rhythms of children, we help our students respond to new learning situations to become even stronger.

Literacy learning is about more than thinking. Literacy learning is also about acting and feeling. At its best, literacy learning incorporates all three intentionally by design. If research shows that the most important way to build deep and sustained memories is to engage our bodies and hearts, we need to intentionally support students to deepen their learning through actions and emotions. Yet, we often focus overwhelmingly on our students' minds during literacy lessons. Sian Beilock (2015), author of *How the Body Knows Its Mind: The Surprising Power of the Physical Environment to Influence How You Think and Feel*, explains: "Our brains don't make that much of a distinction between what happens in your body and what happens in your mind. In fact, our bodies actually hack our brains. The way we move affects our thoughts, our decisions, and our preferences, and kids absorb more when they use their bodies as a learning tool." Beilock is part of the growing field of *embodied cognition*, a new science that illuminates the power of the body and its physical surroundings to shape how we think, feel, and behave.

The Latin root of the word *emotion*, *emovere*, means "to move." Our bodies and minds are linked, and the part of the brain that tells the body to move is adjacent to the part that's responsible for thinking. You may have found in your own life that pacing around the room enhances your creativity; that walking in nature boosts your concentration skills; and that when you work out, you feel stronger physically and mentally. Beilock further explains, "Your body helps you learn, understand, and make sense of the world. It can influence and even change your mind—whether or not you are aware of its influence" (7). When we learn, our minds are processing interactions between our brain, body, and experiences, especially emotional experiences. It's not just that we need the body to show emotions—emotion itself can be traced back to the body.

Art Glenberg (2004, 2007) is a researcher whose motto is "Argo Ergo Cogito"—"I act, therefore I think." Glenberg recruited first and second graders to work in different reading groups; some children were assigned to an "action" reading group while others engaged in repeated oral reading of a text. In the action group students took turns reading sentences aloud, and when they saw a green light at the end of a sentence, they acted out the event in each sentence using simple objects set in front of them. What happened? Beilock explains that the children who acted out the story had a better understanding of the content than the kids who simply read the sentences a second time. Those children also tended to remember a lot more of the details even several days after that initial reading experience.

Glenberg et al. (2004, 2007) found not just small differences. Rather, the students who acted out sentences had increased understanding of the story by 50 percent or more. By acting out the sentences, the children were able to more strongly connect words to the world around them. Actions give words meaning. Beilock (2015) advocates for a more dynamic, interactive context necessary for learning language. She also discusses how "modern neuroscience has yet to find anything like an abstract completely isolated reading area in the brain. Rather, when we read, we tend to activate the same sensory and motor brain areas involved in doing what we are reading about . . . It's hard to separate the reading mind from the doing mind" (50). If it is hard to separate the reading mind from the doing mind, we strengthen students' capacity for remembering and applying key literacy concepts and skills when we design for intentional movement.

DAILY WHOLE-CLASS ROUTINES

We know that the sit-listen-learn model limits students' connections to new texts and new language. Think about your own professional learning experiences. The times you were asked to sit, listen, and learn, you may not have learned very much at all. Rather than spark ideas, this model is a recipe for boredom, disinterest, and disengagement. Yet, when students know that they can count on teachers to incorporate intentional movement and intentional breathing by design, they will quickly look forward to literacy lessons and time when they can count on having their bodies and their minds activated. Rituals that students look forward to as a part of learning where they can incorporate movements at very specific times help make our classrooms happier and our students lives happier.

There are many different literacy learning structures that can incorporate movement and mindful breathing intentionally by design to help students tap into their mind-body connection. The following chart gives a few examples:

Read-Aloud	Find key moments in the text to have students quickly act out a word, a character's action, characters' interactions, or a character's emotion.
Transition to Minilesson	Have students do a quick power pose of their choice so that they are ready to learn something new from a place of power.
Transition to Independent or Partner Reading	Have students engage in intentional breathing for one minute with you modeling how to breathe in and out slowly and purposefully. Emphasize the value of quiet, calm, stillness.
Transition to Independent or Collaborative Writing	Have students engage in a quick, active movement by clapping, jumping, twisting, dabbing, or pickling to wake up their bodies, their senses, and their minds.

When we design for our students' happiness as a part of literacy learning, we can feel confident incorporating these intentional whole-class methods. Students will come to know what to expect and will be able to monitor when to activate with high energy and when to slow down and find calm stillness. By helping students notice the strength in their bodies, they will feel strength in their minds.

SMALL-GROUP MOVEMENT TO STRENGTHEN COMPREHENSION

Glenberg and colleagues' (2004, 2007) research on the value of incorporating movement and gestures into small-group instruction can be simple to put into practice. As with read-alouds, we can preview texts to look for key moments where students can think of their own movement or gesture to strengthen their comprehension of texts. Glenberg and colleagues' research was focused on gestures following individual sentences. In his work, his team used small icons at the end of each sentence where students were expected to think of a small action or gesture to help them make sense of what just happened in the text. We can apply this technique by using little flag sticky notes and inserting them into small-group texts at places where a small action or gesture would help students make meaning of the text.

If adding icons to small-group texts is cumbersome, incorporate a brief sound at the end of sentences where students can go back and reread the sentence and think of a quick action or gesture. Like the icons or sticky notes, this takes some advance planning. This works as a technique when we are reading aloud or modeling with a small group or when students are reading aloud select sentences either to you in a conference or aloud with their group mates. One simple sound technique is to tap the table or your knee as a way to signal to students that this is a sentence to reread and create a small action or gesture for as a pathway to deeper meaning. Incorporating just two or three intentional movement moments into small-group instruction to heighten students' comprehension of instructional texts is purposeful and highly joyful. Once students are comfortable with this small-group routine, students can be invited to find sentences that they think are important to create a small action or gesture for as a pathway to meaning to share with one another, giving them leadership opportunities as part of their learning.

CORE MUSCLES HELP CORE SKILLS

Our core muscles are the body's greatest physical source of strength. The core muscles are the many different muscles in the abdomen and back that work together to support your spine and hold you upright. Your core muscles help you stand strong and tall. They help you lift objects safely. They help counter fatigue and increase our body's endurance. They are also vital for classroom performance. Think about all of the time children are asked to sit at desks and on the classroom rug. Without a strong, stable base, these positions become physically taxing on our students. Energy is depleted and learning becomes hard.

Additionally, strengthening core muscles helps both gross and fine motor skills that are necessary for success as readers and writers. So what can we do? One of the simplest techniques for incorporating intentional core strengthening is to invite students to do reading, writing, or word-sorting activities lying down on their stomachs propped on their elbows. This activates the same muscles needed for planks and the same muscles babies develop when they engage in tummy time. This position offers students further benefits if they need to cross over their midline to retrieve objects such as letter tiles or various pencils. Crossing the body's midline is an important developmental skill. We cross over our midline when we scratch an elbow and cross our ankles. We also cross over our midline when we read from left to right. So giving students physical opportunities to cross their midlines in joyful ways helps strengthen the brain's pathways that will help them read from left to right with greater ease. Our motor and cognitive skills are linked, so intentionally designing for students to have options in how they use their bodies with the midline in mind helps them grow in a myriad of ways. Occupational therapists have a wealth of knowledge about the body and the connection between crossing the midline and academic skills.

Every child's profile is different. Both of my sons were highly motivated in preschool to get across the monkey bars. They could swim across a pool safely at a young age. They fell in love with planks for some reason unknown to me. They also mastered tying their shoes without much adult support. Yet, they lacked confidence learning to ride a bike. Learning to write lowercase letters was a challenge. Their stamina for writing was not as strong as many of their peers. At the recommendation of preschool teachers, both of my boys did sessions with a masterful occupational therapist who taught me so much about incorporating movement and the body into learning. I had been a teacher of children and adults for almost twenty years, and I had none of the knowledge the OT had. I was learning as a parent what I should have known as a teacher—movement is a human need and in many cases can boost learning.

If you have an OT in your building, buddy up. Schedule time to learn from their expertise in intentional movement as a part of learning not just for children who qualify for occupational therapy services but so that all of your students can benefit.

LEADERSHIP JOBS THAT INVITE KIDS TO MOVE

Some of our most active students on the playground can also be some of our most frustrated students on a classroom rug when their bodies are expected to be still but they have built-up energy. Observing your students throughout the day both inside and outside classroom spaces will give you a quick sense of who would benefit from literacy jobs that foster movement as well as leadership. When students can use their bodies to help others in the classroom, they are positioned as leaders rather than distractions. Consider giving certain students permanent jobs that help them channel their movements around the classroom in positive way. Students who benefit from heavy lifting can be in charge of carrying book bins. They can help stack chairs or move tables into new positions. Students who benefit from movement at the start and end of independent practice time can be in charge of distributing supplies to tables around the room. Students who benefit from letting their voices out can be invited to help you make midworkshop announcements. The truth is many students will tune in more to their classmate's voice more than yours. As you consider your students' strengths and their movement needs, look for ways to craft leadership opportunities that honor our students' natural tendencies and use positive framing as a way to build self-efficacy and a sense of pride in students. They will carry those experiences with them forever.

DESIGN FOR MOVEMENT

- Notice your students' natural rhythms as you consider ways to incorporate movement and breathing exercises by design.
- Plan moments during read-alouds for students to use a gesture, show a facial expression, or quickly act out a moment from the text—look for powerful verbs, figurative language, and rich description.
- Incorporate movement into vocabulary and academic language instruction through gestures that build mental models of new terms, role playing, and dramatic interpretation of words and concepts.
- Have students create a personal power pose (see Invitations, page 171) as a strategy for feeling powerful during transitional moments.
- Incorporate quick active movements to wake up students' bodies, senses, and minds especially before something collaborative or activity-driven.
- Teach students "joy breathing" strategies that you can use as a class during transition times before literacy learning that requires calm or stillness; encourage students to use these strategies on their own when they need them.
- Plan for movement in small-group instruction by previewing texts with movement in mind—use an icon or a sound to indicate for students when a movement can help them better imagine the situation the character is in.
- Build students' core muscles by giving them options for reading, writing, or engaging in word sorting on their stomachs, on stools, or on yoga balls rather than at their seats.
- Incorporate manipulatives like letter tiles and sentence strips that give students reasons to cross their midline to retrieve objects.
- Look for leadership opportunities for students who would benefit from additional movement or additional speaking opportunities; use positive framing to reposition children's movement needs as a strength rather than a deficit.

Chapter 9

Becoming a Designer

> ## The ultimate source of happiness is within us.
>
> —His Holiness, The Dalai Lama

GETTING STARTED

It is my hope that this book will be an invitation to more joy and happiness for you and your students. The seven pillars are designed to help you transform your teaching so that happiness is an enduring trait of your literacy instruction. With new discoveries in neuroscience and psychology, we now have profound insights into human flourishing and sustainable happiness. Rooted in the science of happiness, this book offers you a path for making your literacy instruction memorable, purposeful, and joy driven for students. You know that we can teach happiness and that we can design for it. Becoming a designer of student happiness as a part of literacy learning means being intentional in your planning, instruction, methods, and language choices. Knowing where to start can be a challenge. This chapter offers some suggestions for small changes you can make right away. Make small changes by maximizing the first five minutes of instruction and by ensuring that you make time for the last five minutes of instruction. This is the kind of teaching we tend to do on the fly rather than by design. But how we invite students into their learning and how we bring closure to each learning session matters. The following section offers some ideas for how to keep going with making happiness a priority in your classroom especially when you face an onslaught of new initiatives. Instead of feeling like happiness is "one more thing," make teaching toward happiness a priority. Let happiness be your true north. Start with joy by starting small.

Small Things Often

Change usually doesn't happen because of one big thing we do. Instead, change happens because of all the small things we do over time with consistency. One motto I try to remember in life and in my classroom is that "small things often can create big changes over time." The following sections will give you some ideas for how to get started by focusing on the small things you can do every day starting now. It doesn't matter if you are in the middle of a unit or the middle of a great read-aloud. It doesn't matter if you are alone in making these shifts to your practice to make happiness a priority in your classroom. You won't be alone for long.

Making Connections

Every day students are looking to connect with you and to one another. Some of our students who present themselves as the most disconnected need connection the most. Times in my life when I have felt happiest are when I know I am in a community where I am valued and where I never have to question whether I am in the company of people who care. This starts at a very young age for all of us. The more we can strengthen the sense of connection for our students as early as possible, the more they will feel self-worth and strive to learn for themselves. So how can you make connection a priority right now as a part of literacy learning? Here are a few quick, get-started ideas:

- Greet students at the door. Shake their hands. Look them in the eye. Tell them you are so happy to see them today.
- Create a class handshake or high-five routine.
- Ask students the names and nicknames they want to be called by.
- Use a class list to track the ways you recognize students in a positive way during the literacy block.
- Read the books your students are choosing to read.
- Offer a variety of reading materials to tap into students' interests: magazines, graphic novels, picture books, nonfiction titles, fantasy, science fiction, realistic fiction, historical fiction, and poetry.
- Follow the children's books that children themselves are voting for by researching the Children's Book Council Children's Choice Selections.
- Create classroom charts for students to write "I Am" and "I Can" statements when they occur to them.
- Build a book talk routine that students opt in to.
- Incorporate morning meeting and closing circle routines where students are encouraged to share something they are proud of or how they helped make others happy that day.
- Give students compliment cards to show them that you see them and the hard work they are putting in to their learning.
- Create a "just because" thank-you-note corner for students to write notes to one another.

- Give students the choice of where they sit each day, and trust them to build a community next to new peers.
- Commit to a turn-and-talk routine every literacy block.
- Share your favorite books with students each week.
- Encourage students to share favorite sentences from their independent reading books.
- Encourage students to share favorite words or sentences from their own writing.
- Play.
- Smile.

Maximizing the First Five Minutes

The first five minutes of instruction have a variety of names and a variety of approaches but tend to fall under the umbrella of planning for your "engagement hook." What will pull students in to the learning in a way that research on learning and happiness supports? Like the start of a good book, the first five minutes of instruction matter in giving students a reason to engage. Maximize the first five minutes of instruction by planning what you will say to get students thinking about what is to come, connecting to what they have previously learned or experienced, or tapping into students' natural curiosity. Some of my favorite ways to start literacy lessons are:

- posing a question that allows students to think about their own life experiences ("Did you ever _____?"; "Think about a time when you _____")
- sharing a brief story from my own life ("I remember when _____"; "One day _____")
- sharing wonder statements ("Lately, I have been wondering _____")
- projecting an image that supports students to make their thinking visible by saying what they see, think, and wonder (famous works of art; comic strips; photos from my own life)
- reflecting on what students have done well and what they should feel proud of lately while also encouraging them to challenge themselves ("I have noticed _____"; "Because _____, you're ready to _____")

Making Time for the Last Five Minutes

Intentionally designing the last five minutes of instruction can be hard particularly when you want to give students enough time to read, write, and try new things. But when we take a step back to think about what students will really remember about the lesson and their experience with it, they are much more likely to remember something that they feel connected to, especially when they have time built in to reflect on their learning. Think about your instruction from the perspective of a whole-small-whole model. If every lesson starts as a whole group for about ten minutes, then students will be set up for success when they are independently practicing new skills and strategies or when they are working collaboratively in a small group. As important as the first few minutes are for building connections, the last five minutes help students transition out of their independent or collaborative practice back to the group as a whole. It's really an opportunity for students to share how their learning went that day.

- Build sharing routines based on the same guiding questions to help solidify the routine and to hear new voices: What went well? What felt good? What was hard? What was unexpected? What surprised them about themselves?
- Keep a class list to record who shares during each closure session so that you can encourage other students to share when they are ready and have something to say.
- Build in time for students to ask questions.
- Build in structures for students to call on one another.
- Have students say in their own words what they feel they learned that session and what they are proud of themselves for as readers, writers, creators, and communicators.
- Encourage students to add to the class "I Am" or "I Can" interactive writing charts as a silent means of reflection.
- Have students revisit their happiness lists in light of things they read, wrote, or created that made them happy.
- Have students reflect on ways they helped others during the literacy block. How did they make someone else happy today?

HOW TO KEEP GOING

Once you decide to prioritize happiness in your classroom as a part of literacy learning, it's helpful to have strategies to keep the happiness momentum going. Think about times in your own life when you committed to something new and how you adjusted your outlook and your actions to keep it going.

When I turned forty, I decided to start a new commitment to exercise and healthy eating. All of the strategies I had tried in the past didn't really work. I went to exercise classes once in a while that seemed to motivate me, but then I would skip for a few weeks and have a hard time getting started again. Or I would prioritize healthy eating, but then when I got busy or stressed, I'd grab pizza because it was convenient and then I'd feel guilty about it afterward. Finally, I decided to make a change after I noticed my friend had radically changed her life by joining a Facebook accountability group led by a positive, joyful, inspiring leader. I started working out every day for half an hour in my basement and I joined a private Facebook group that kept me accountable and inspired. I reached new goals. I felt stronger. I stopped getting sick every couple of weeks. I was a better teacher, friend, parent, and spouse.

As stated earlier, Will Durant wrote, "We are what we repeatedly do." I tend to agree. What we do once in a while doesn't really matter. That doesn't mean special days and celebrations don't matter. They do. But what matters more are the small, everyday choices we make that drive our lives. Once you commit to making happiness a priority in your classroom, it's going to take small choices every day to really change the classroom community and your relationship with your students.

Giving Students a Say

Once you establish the seven pillars as priorities in your classroom and you get started with a focus on small things every day, start to look for ways to give your students more of a say about their learning. Reflect on where your students have choice and agency. Reflect on where they seem most energized and engaged. Reflect on who is doing most of the talking and who needs their voice lifted up. Think about the ways that students contribute, and encourage them to realize there are many ways to "say something." Share with students Peter Reynolds' picture book *Say Something* (2019) as a way to launch a say something initiative that places students' voices and choices as a renewed and explicit priority in your classroom. In the book, there are many different ways students are encouraged to say something through speaking, writing, drawing, creating, organizing, and building. Have students reflect on the ways they feel most comfortable "saying something," and invite students to share their thinking in ways that go beyond verbal or written responses.

You can also look for opportunities for students to have a say by giving the class agency in some instructional decision making such as voting on the next read-aloud, signing up for book talk days, signing up for the sharing of poetry, and creating class rubrics or giving students a chance to critique and alter existing rubrics. Ask students times when they feel like they should have a say and listen to your students' ideas. Try your best to honor the ones that you can.

Kidwatching

At its simplest, kidwatching is exactly like it sounds: watching kids as they engage as readers, writers, communicators, collaborators, and creators. Yetta Goodman (1985) popularized the term in her book *Kidwatching: Observing Children in the Classroom* where she explains the practice of kidwatching as "watching kids with a knowledgeable head" (9). Kidwatching is an opportunity to prioritize your own inquiry stance about the students in your classroom. It's an intentional time where you devote your focus to noticing and wondering about your students, how they learn, what they do as they explore their ideas and as they interact with each other. Mills (2005) explains it as an instructional strategy based on "a seek-to-understand stance by attempting to look at life, literacy, and learning through the children's eyes" (2).

To maximize what you observe when you focus on kidwatching, create a simple tool that will help you keep track of what you see, think, and wonder about your students. Something like the following chart can allow you to notice and wonder about students regardless of what they are engaged in as learners:

Date _____   Time of Day _____
Activity/Lesson: _____

Student	I See	I Think	I Wonder

Use this same format as a way to look beyond what is observable in class and gather artifacts that help you build a more comprehensive sense of your students: writing samples, reader response notebooks, drawings, exit slips, audio or video recordings.

If we are what we repeatedly do, then kidwatching once in a while will make it hard to build a consistent routine for yourself. You do not need to observe every student every day but consider committing to jotting down observations about five students each week or each student once a month as a way to commit to taking a step back to take notice of things that traditionally you might not see about your students. Consider the benefit of kidwatching outside of instructional time such as joining your students on the playground or in the cafeteria or in P.E. class to see your students in a new way. When we prioritize kidwatching as a means of teaching toward happiness, we give ourselves a new way of focusing on how students learn rather than on what they know or are able to do.

Share your kidwatching notes with colleagues during planning session, and use them as a tool for thinking about the ways your students seem to be energized and engaged in their learning and where you can make instructional changes to keep energy and engagement high.

Prioritizing Your Own Happiness Routines

Literacy researchers Anthony Applegate and Mary Dekonty Applegate (2004) found in their groundbreaking study that teachers who are engaged and enthusiastic readers are more likely to encourage and cultivate those same stances toward reading in their students. But they began to wonder about their preservice students; what if a significant number of teachers did not have a love of reading themselves? They recalled the story of Apostle Peter who, when asked for money by a beggar, stated that he could not give what he did not have. They coined the term the "Peter Effect" for thinking about the same scenario for teachers as readers.

But what if the same principle applied to teachers' happiness? Teachers who are charged with supporting students to find their own happiness must also have ways of finding happiness for themselves. Research on teacher burnout and retention shows us that classroom tensions can be contagious and that teachers who have higher levels of burnout had students with higher levels of stress hormones each morning. Additionally, half a million (15 percent) of U.S. teachers leave the profession every year (Seidel 2014). Further, TNTP (formerly The New Teacher Project) reported almost 66 percent of the nation's best teachers continue to leave the profession for careers elsewhere (Chartock and Wiener 2014). Although resources and class composition will differ from school to school and classroom to classroom, you can take steps to prioritize happiness in your life so that you in turn can contribute to sustainable happiness for your students.

- Find "joy friends" or people in your building that make you smile and laugh.
- Commit to your own five-minute journaling routine.
- Keep your own happiness list and add to it once a week.
- Practice breathing strategies so that you can teach them to your students.
- Focus on seeing the good in all situations.
- Join a Facebook accountability group focused on teaching, wellness, or exercise.

- Get outside and reconnect with nature.
- Prioritize your break time, and know that when you use it to connect with colleagues, you are doing something good for yourself and your students.
- Set goals for yourself as a teacher by focusing on the small things you can change every day, right now.
- Prioritize feelings of play in your own life.
- Turn on away messages for work over the weekends.
- Track your personal screen time and commit to reducing screen time each week so that you can refocus on presence.
- Turn off the inner voice that is your biggest critic and turn up the inner voice that is your biggest cheerleader.
- Write your own "I Am" and "I Can" statements.
- Find joy in your own reading and writing life.
- Smile and introduce yourself to strangers (see what happens).
- Share stories from your life with those around you.

Ask Yourself: "What Will Students Really Remember?"

Thanks to the wonders of social media, a former student of mine reconnected with me after almost twenty years. He was in my fourth-grade class the first year I had my own classroom. Shawn was a recent immigrant from Taiwan, and he lived with his sister, father, and grandmother. His mom had died from cancer when he was two years old, and he had virtually no memory of her. Shawn walked into my classroom with limited English exposure but with the compassion to be kind to himself and those around him. When I knew Shawn, he was nine years old, and when we reconnected, he was almost thirty. By then, he was running a highly successful and well-known restaurant in Manhattan.

When I received his message, I went down to my basement to the plastic bins of student work I've kept over the years and I found his shape poems, his letter to 9/11 rescue workers, and his water conservation letter to President Bush. I mailed him these pieces of writing from his nine-year-old self with a letter about how much he had changed me as a teacher and how often I thought of him over the years. We corresponded for a few months and it reaffirmed for me all that I know students remember most about our short time with them. More than reading or writing strategies. More than the books we read. More than the projects we create. They will remember the feelings of unconditional love. They will remember how we supported them in times of challenge. They will remember how we lifted them up with our hope.

When you are feeling uncertain about what is the right thing to do, ask yourself, "What will students really remember?" Every teacher I know that has made a positive impact on children's lives has their own Shawn. They have several. You never know the influence you have on someone else's life. My greatest hope is that all children find happiness in their lives and that school becomes a place where children know they can outgrow the best version of themselves. Join me. Become a designer. Start with joy.

Part 2

INVITATIONS

Happiness can be found in the darkest
of times, if one only remembers
to turn on the light.

—Albus Dumbledore, in J. K. Rowling, *Harry Potter and the Prisoner of Azkaban*

There are times in our teaching when we need to turn on the light and reclaim joy to make literacy instruction a source of happiness for us, and, most importantly, for our students. The following invitations are possibilities for lessons that can give your literacy instruction a boost to help students find purpose and meaning in what they are learning. These invitations are also designed to help you and your students reclaim joy when you find you need it most. When we start to focus on small moments of joy, we build the roots for something much bigger in our lives and in our students' lives: sustained happiness. These lessons are designed as supplements to the robust and important strategy work or genre studies your students are engaged in. In addition, these invitations are designed with research in mind to support students to make connections, consider their choices, rise to new challenges, be playful, discover new things about themselves and the world, share their stories, move with intention, and know wholeheartedly that their best is always enough.

INVITATIONS

1. The Best Part of Me (Literature Spotlight: *The Best Part of Me: Children Talk About Their Bodies in Words and Pictures* by Wendy Ewald)

2. What Do I Notice and Wonder (About Me?) (Literature Spotlight: *What Do You Do with an Idea?*, *What Do You Do with a Problem?* and *What Do You Do with a Chance?* by Kobi Yamada)

3. What Makes Me Feel Strong? (Literature Spotlight: *After the Fall: How Humpty Dumpty Got Back Up Again* by Dan Santat)

4. Power Poses (Literature Spotlight: *The Word Collector* by Peter Reynolds)

5. Closely Reading Characters to Closely Read Me and You (Literature Spotlight: *Why Am I Me?* by Paige Britt)

6. I Am, I Can, I Did (Literature Spotlight: *Lost and Found* by Oliver Jeffers)

7. Hmm . . . Yes, And; Yes, But; No, Because (Literature Spotlight: *Wolf in the Snow* by Matt Cordell)

8. Three Good Things (Literature Spotlight: *Extra Yarn* by Mac Barnett)

9. Asking Questions Gets Us to Better Questions (Literature Spotlight: *The Antlered Ship* by Dashka Slater)

10. Listening with Love (Literature Spotlight: *The Rabbit Listened* by Cori Doerrfeld)

INVITATION 1
The Best Part of Me

When our students look in the mirror, do they see their biggest cheerleader or their harshest critic? Not only does sharing parts of themselves make students more socially connected, it strengthens their belief that they are worthy of love and belonging—all essential components of sustainable happiness.

This invitation is designed to help students think about the best parts of themselves. The best parts of themselves could be a part of their body as many children have done in Wendy Ewald's incredible photographic poetry collection *The Best Part of Me: Children Talk About Their Bodies in Words and Pictures* (2002). But students could also think about their best parts by considering other qualities in themselves that they love: their laughter, dreams, friendship, confidence, curiosity, or hope.

WARM UP: *Set the stage by letting students know writers often write from their own lives.*

As writers, our everyday lives give us possibilities for what to write about. We know that lots of good stories have problems and solutions. But not every kind of writing needs to be about problems. Our lives are full of joyful things that are worthy of writing about, starting with us!

TEACH: *Support students to think about something they love about themselves as a starting place for writing. Model with your own example.*

When you think about yourself, what are all of the things you love about yourself? Close your eyes and think for a minute about all the best parts of you. When you have some ideas, open your eyes. I hope you had a lot of things you were picturing in your mind. I decided to write about one of the best parts of me—my laughter. (Share your own example.)

TRY: *Have students turn and talk to a partner or sketch/ jot an idea.*

> *Take another moment and think back to the things you pictured in your mind that are the best parts of you. Now narrow down your thinking to one idea you want to put into writing today.*

CLARIFY: *Remind students that writers write from their own lives to express what they love about themselves.*

> *As writers, you are going to write about many things in your life. Today, I want you to focus on something positive that you love about yourself. Remember, it can be something on your body like your hair, your feet, your smile, your eyes, or anything else. But, it can also be something we can't see like your laughter, your confidence, your curiosity, or your kindness.*

TEACHER TIPS

Some students will be able to take to the page right away with an idea about the best parts of themselves. Other students may need some additional conferring. You may want to encourage students to take photos of parts of themselves they love, if they choose something you can see as a way of starting with a different means of expression other than writing. You may also want students to gather ideas from their classmates about what they think the best part of them is, especially if they are hesitant at first. The goal is to make everyone feel included and worthy of belonging.

If students need more support taking to the page, consider this multistep process and writing frame:

**Think about the things you love most
about yourself that you want others to know.**

Start by listing all the things you love about yourself.

Then, put a star next to the thing you most love about yourself that you want others to know.

Next, make a list of all the reasons why you love that about yourself.

Finally, through writing and drawing, explain to others what you love most about yourself and why.

I love about myself:

Why I love that about myself:

For students that benefit from sentence frames consider something like:

The best part of me is _____ because _____.

My _____ is/are _____.

My _____ is/are as _____ as _____.

Without my _____, I wouldn't be able to _____.

The best part of me is _____ because _____.

LITERATURE SUGGESTIONS

In addition to Wendy Ewald's book, I love pairing this lesson with *Why Am I Me?* by Paige Britt (2017) and *Same, Same, but Different* by Jenny Sue Kostecki-Shaw (2011). Any of the picture books mentioned in these invitations help students recognize that our identities help shape who we are, how we feel about ourselves, and how we can come to understand others.

In addition to reading books alongside this lesson, consider creating a class book that features all of your students' Best Part of Me pieces and artwork. This will quickly become a prized classroom possession.

INVITATION 2
What Do I Notice and Wonder (About Me?)

We won't love every book we pick up and read. Nor should we be expected to. Our students are the same way. With so many books in the world, we want our students to select books that make them feel something, that offer them something new, or that allow them to feel proud. That means we have to give students space to make choices, which can start with helping them tap into what they notice and wonder about themselves as readers. When do they feel excited as readers? When do they feel frustrated or bored? When do they want to tell someone else about what they've read? When do they notice they are full of questions? Tapping into these observations about ourselves can be really helpful in shaping our book choices. Also, giving space for students to share these observations about themselves with others lets them know that it's okay to have mixed experiences as readers. Here is some suggested language for this lesson. The specific word choices matter less than the intention of giving students an opportunity to think about their own experiences as readers and to voice their opinions.

WARM UP: *Set the stage by letting students know readers feel differently about different books.*

As readers, there are lots of times when we'll feel excited about what we are reading. There will even be times when we feel so proud of ourselves because we've read something new, challenging, or unfamiliar. But there are other times when what we are reading doesn't interest us so much. Or we might feel frustrated that the book doesn't feel like a good fit. Sometimes a book might even be boring to us but be really interesting to someone else.

TEACH: *Support students to pay attention to what they notice about their own reading experience today as well as what they wonder. Model with your own example.*

While you are reading, pay attention to what you notice and wonder about yourself as a reader today. You might notice how the book makes you feel about the characters or even about yourself. Were you surprised at any point? You might notice that you love the words the author uses or the illustrations. You might notice you want to read more books like this one. Or you might notice the opposite of those feelings. You might wonder if there are other books like this one or who you can talk to about this book.

TRY: *Have students bring a collection of books they are reading. These are sometimes in book baggies, book boxes, or their desks.*

Take a look at the books you've chosen recently in a pile in front of you. Take a look at the covers and think to yourself a moment: What do I notice about my reaction to these books? Is there anything I wonder about these books or myself thanks to these books? When you have an idea, turn and talk to someone seated near you to share your thinking.

CLARIFY: *Remind students that there are so many books in the world and that it's helpful to pay attention to their own reactions to books.*

As readers, there are some books that will make us feel excited, proud, or that make us laugh out loud. Those are all joyful feelings. There are other times when quite honestly we will feel bored or even frustrated. That's okay. The world is full of amazing books just waiting to be found by you. Today, remember to pay attention to what you notice and wonder about yourself while you are reading.

TEACHER TIPS

This lesson is helpful to teach either before or after a lesson on noticing and wondering using images. Learning to use the language associated with noticing and wondering is a helpful device for students to say more and make their thinking visible. Although there is much to notice and wonder about a text, it's also valuable to give students permission to notice and wonder things about themselves as readers.

LITERATURE SUGGESTIONS

I love the picture book trilogy written by Kobi Yamada (2014, 2016, 2018) and illustrated by Mae Besom: *What Do You Do with an Idea?*, *What Do You Do with a Problem?* and *What Do You Do with a Chance?* These are great books for modeling the power of wondering and human resilience. Sometimes we have problems and we have to figure out how to solve them. Sometimes we have ideas but we doubt that they are worthy of sharing with others. Sometimes we are given a chance and we're not sure whether we are brave enough to take it. There are a myriad of ways you can use these books, but they can also be used as companion texts for this lesson. The main character is consistent across the books, and each time he experiences something new, he has to figure out what to do about it. A lot of parallels can be made to students and their lives including their reading and writing lives. If we want readers to live inspired reading lives, then these are powerful books to spark a culture of joyful literacy.

INVITATION 3
What Makes Me Feel Strong?

This invitation is designed to help students realize their strengths, by reflecting on the things that make them feel strong as readers, writers, speakers, listeners, or creators, and to share those with others. It is especially important for students to recognize that when we experience setbacks, we can draw on our strengths to get back up again as Humpty Dumpty does in Dan Santat's (2014) *After the Fall: How Humpty Dumpty Got Back Up Again*. Humpty Dumpty does not stay broken. Rather, he gets back up again to respond to not only the physical trauma but also the emotional trauma that came from the fall. He does so by regaining some enjoyment in life. He taps into what makes him feel strong.

WARM UP: *Invite students to picture in their minds a time they felt strong.*

> *Close your eyes and picture in your mind a time when you felt really strong. Think about who you were with and what you were doing. Did you say anything out loud? How did you feel? Open your eyes and turn and talk to the person seated near you what you were imagining.*

TEACH: *Model how we can be strong as readers, writers, speakers, listeners, or creators.*

> *We are strong in lots of different ways in our lives. Did you know we can be strong as readers, writers, speakers, listeners, and creators? We are strong every time we surprise ourselves. We are strong every time we try something new. We are strong every time we go first at something even when we are nervous.* (Share your own literacy-related examples.)

TRY: *Invite students to share their thinking for a class chart using either shared or interactive writing.*

> *As learners, we are all strong in different ways. Let's think together about all the ways we are strong as readers, writers, speakers, listeners, and creators and make a class chart about our ideas.*

CLARIFY: *Remind students that every day is a chance to feel strong as a literacy learner.*

While you are reading/writing, think about what makes you feel strong today. Did you try something new, or did you surprise yourself with your own strength? I'll be coming around to hear from you all about the ways you feel strong today, and I'll also be on the lookout for ways I think you are strong every day.

TEACHER TIPS

Many students will initially associate strength with something physical. That's okay. This lesson uses that association but helps them move beyond it to consider the ways they are strong as literacy learners. The goal of the lesson is to help students identify the strengths they have in themselves every time they:

> surprise themselves
>
> try something new
>
> go first at something.

Use moments of observation of your students to notice the ways they seem strong to you and let them know you see them at their strongest.

LITERATURE SUGGESTIONS

I love *After the Fall: How Humpty Dumpty Got Back Up Again* by Dan Santat for its clever twist on a traditional story. Pairing *After the Fall* with any character-driven story where the main character is motivated to try something new is going to be a worthwhile read. Some of my favorite fiction picture books to build motivation and a positive self-image include: *Jabari Jumps* by Gaia Cornwall (2017), *I Am Enough* by Grace Byers (2018), *The Thing Lou Couldn't Do* by Ashley Spires (2017), *What to Do with a Box* by Jane Yolen (2016), *What Do You Do with a Chance?* by Kobi Yamada (2018), *Stuck* by Oliver Jeffers (2001), *Samson in the Snow* by Philip Stead (2016), and *The Wolf, the Duck, and the Mouse* by Mac Barnett (2017).

Biographies also provide a myriad of powerful life stories to help students tap into their strengths and try new things, such as: *Little Leaders: Bold Women in Black History* by Vashti Harrison (2017), *Shaking Things Up: 14 Young Women Who*

Changed the World by Susan Hood (2018), *Hidden Figures: The True Story of Four Black Women and the Space Race* by Margot Lee Shetterly (2018), *Mae Among the Stars* by Roda Ahmed (2018), *Separate Is Never Equal: Sylvia Mendez and Her Family's Fight for Desegregation* by Duncan Tonatiuh (2014), *Brave Girl: Clara and the Shirtwaist Makers' Strike of 1909* by Michelle Markel (2013).

INVITATION 4
Power Poses

This invitation is designed to tap into students' bodies as a way to help them feel strong as learners. It's also based on research from the field of embodied psychology and specifically the work of Amy Cuddy (2015) from her book *Presence*. Our bodies shape our minds, and when we make ourselves small, our thinking can feel small. When we make ourselves big and powerful, we start to believe that our ideas are powerful, too. We see people in power poses when their arms reach up in the air, when runners cross a finish line, or when someone stands with their hands on their hips. The cover image from *The Word Collector* by Peter Reynolds (2018) is an example of a child in a power pose with a clear association to the power of words and wondering.

WARM UP: *Invite students to notice and name what they see and think about images of people in power poses.*

Let's look at some images of people in different kinds of poses. What do you notice about these people? What does it make you think? Turn and talk to a partner to share what you see and think. Give students a few moments to share their thinking with a partner, and then invite students to share their thinking about the images with the larger group.

TEACH: *Model how we can use our bodies to shape our minds.*

You all have a lot of important ideas about what you notice about the people in these pictures and what it makes you think. There's a special word for all of the ways these people are using their bodies—they are all in power poses. A power pose is when you use your body to make yourself feel strong. (Model a few power poses for students. Explain why power poses help us feel strong and how they make our ideas even stronger.)

TRY: *Invite students to stand up as a group and try a power pose.*

Now it's your turn. Right where you are, stand up, and get your body into a power pose . . . Wow, we have all chosen lots of different poses that help us feel strong. (After a moment, invite students to share how the power pose made them feel with a partner. This will help transition students from being up and in their pose to back down and ready to transfer this concept to the learning they're about to do as readers or writers.)

CLARIFY: *Remind students that they can get into a power pose when they need a moment to make themselves feel strong.*

Today or any day, you can take a small moment to get yourself into a power pose to help you feel strong. That might happen at the end of reading or writing today. It might happen when you are struggling with something and want a little boost.

TEACHER TIPS

When we build students' energy up, we need a way to bring it back down before we transition to independent practice or learning that requires more stillness and quiet. Consider transitioning from power posing to reading aloud *The Word Collector* by Peter Reynolds as a way to support students to notice the ways that the cover image shows the main character, Jerome, in a power pose and how he uses that positive energy throughout the story to do something positive for himself and the world. Use Jerome as an example of what it means to be a curious, strong reader, writer, thinker, and communicator.

LITERATURE SUGGESTIONS

In addition to *The Word Collector* by Peter Reynolds (2018), I also love using books like Susan Verde's *I Am Love: A Book of Compassion* (2019), *I Am Human: A Book of Empathy* (2018), *I Am Peace: A Book of Mindfulness* (2017), and *I Am Yoga* (2015) all illustrated by Peter Reynolds. This set of books is full of illustrated examples of the importance of the body-mind connection, and each book offers students a narrative that will help strengthen their memory for the concept. I also love books like *Rosie Revere, Engineer* by Andrea Beaty (2013), *Salt in His Shoes* by Deloris and Roslyn Jordan (2000), *Whistle for Willie* by Ezra Jack Keats (1964), and *The Thing Lou Couldn't Do* by Ashley Spires (2017), which all have illustrations where children are in a variety of poses that serve as mentors for power posing in the world.

INVITATION 5
Closely Reading Characters to Closely Read Me and You

"Why am I me?" may be the most profound question we ask ourselves throughout our entire lives. It's also the eponymous question in Paige Britt's (2017) picture book collaboration with illustrators Sean Qualls and Selina Alko. In this spare, yet illuminating book, two children see each other on a train and wonder to themselves: "Why am I me . . . and not you? Why are you, you . . . and not me?"

In this invitation, students are supported to closely read characters as a pathway for closely reading themselves and eventually others. This is a great opportunity to support students through the thinking strategy I see, I think, I wonder.

WARM UP: *Invite students to consider the questions: Why am I me? and What makes me, me?*

Ask these open-ended questions as a way to spark students' thinking about themselves first. Let them know there are not simple answers to these questions but that they are important ones to ask.

Hmmm . . . sometimes I wonder to myself, Why am I me? *and* What makes me, me? *Sometimes thinking about characters and all of the things that make them who they are helps me think about myself and even helps me think about the people I meet in my life in new ways.*

TEACH: *Model for students your own thinking about characters on the cover of* Why Am I Me? *or another book that sparks conversations about identity, community, and being human (see following suggestions).*

(Model for students your thinking about something you see, think, and wonder about the cover of a picture book you plan on using in this lesson. You may want to focus your modeling on what you notice and wonder about the characters' interests.)

Let's look at this cover together. I'm going to use three sentence starters to help me share what I'm thinking: I see, I think, I wonder.

TRY: *Invite students to share something on a class chart that uses the thinking prompts: I see, I think, I wonder.*

> *Let's grow our thinking by hearing some of your ideas about what you see, think, and wonder about these characters.*

CLARIFY: *Remind students that they can closely read characters in stories, but they can also take the time to closely read themselves and all the people in life they meet.*

> *How can this strategy help us think about ourselves and what makes us, us? How can this strategy help us think about new people we might meet in life or even one another here in this class?*

TEACHER TIPS

The thinking strategy I see, I think, I wonder has incredible versatility and is a way for students to express their noticings and wonderings about illustrations, other images, multimedia, and print text. It's also a way for students to start noticing and wondering to ask bigger questions where there is no singular or certain answer about who we are, where we're from, and why we are here. Use this lesson as a pathway to continued conversations about identity, community, and humanity throughout the year.

LITERATURE SUGGESTIONS

There are many books that can open conversations about identity, community, and being human. In addition to *Why Am I Me?* the following titles can help open up such conversations with young learners: *Same, Same but Different* by Jenny Sue Kostecki-Shaw (2011), *Same Sun Here* by Silas House and Neela Vaswani (2012), *Most People* by Michael Leannah (2017), *Lovely* by Jess Hong (2017), *No One Else Like You* by Siska Goeminne (2017), *The Colors of Us* by Karen Katz (1999), *Whoever You Are* by Mem Fox (1997), *Skin Again* by bell hooks (2004), *Shades of People* by Sheila M. Kelly (2009), and *Let's Talk About Race* by Julius Lester (2008). Support students to make connections as you read across the books focused on the great diversity of people in the world.

INVITATION 6
I Am, I Can, I Did

This invitation is designed to encourage students to add to ongoing class concept maps that give them a space to use writing in a public way to name something affirmational about themselves, to name what they can do, and to feel proud about something they did do. This lesson launches the process for students to self-select when it is a good time for them to add to an interactive class chart on large display paper. Every student may not immediately have an idea to add, but over time all of your students will add to these displays. Hang these charts somewhere where students can access them, and place a jar of inviting thin markers nearby for students to add to the charts when an idea strikes them.

Although many picture books could be used to help students reflect not only on themselves but also on compelling characters, *Lost and Found* by Oliver Jeffers (2005) is a story of setbacks, perseverance, friendship, and hope. Beautifully illustrated, this imaginative story describes what happens when a penguin shows up on a boy's doorstep and he assumes the penguin must be lost. What he realizes in the end is that all along the penguin just wanted to be found.

WARM UP: *Invite students to think about the things that make them who they are and all that they have accomplished so far in the school year inside and outside of school.*

> *Every day I see the incredible things you are doing to outgrow yourself and to become the best version of you possible. Think for a moment about something you have done so far this year that you are especially proud of either in school or outside of school. Hold that thought in your mind.*

TEACH: *Model how we can use language to think about the traits that make us who we are and the ways that writing down something positive about ourselves helps us feel strong throughout the day.*

> *You've been doing a lot of new things this year. It's helpful to take time to reflect on the things that make us who we are and what we have achieved together. There are three phrases that can help us gather our thoughts to share them with one another today but throughout the year:* "I Am," "I Can," "I Did." (Have three different chart papers

with each of these written in the middle. Model your own thinking across each of these sentence starters with an example from your own life.)

TRY: *Invite students to record their thinking about one of these statements on the chart paper.*

Now it's your turn. If you already have an "I Am," "I Can," "I Did" thought that you want to add to the chart, there are markers next to each chart when you feel you have something to write.

CLARIFY: *Remind students that these charts will be an invitation for them to add to whenever they have an idea.*

These charts will be hung in a place you can reach, and you'll always find markers nearby so that you can add to these whenever you have something new that you want to record. You'll have to ask yourself whether it feels like the right time to add something, but I trust that you will make a good decision, and I can't wait to see what ideas you have that you want to share.

TEACHER TIPS

This is a great invitation to use before introducing character traits. A follow-up lesson to this invitation is to have students write "I Am," "I Can," "I Did" statements for the characters they meet either in read-alouds or in their own independent reading. This helps simplify the thinking involved in naming character traits or thinking more deeply about characters. Rather than overcomplicating that thought process, linking this invitation to characters helps students make a natural connection from themselves to the characters they meet in books.

LITERATURE SUGGESTIONS

Absolutely any high-quality, character-driven story will work as a way to bridge this invitation on self-literacy to the understandings students are forming about characters. Some of my favorites include Oliver Jeffers' *Lost and Found* and Philip Stead's (2010) *A Sick Day for Amos McGee*. In both of these books, the characters are complex, although the story lines are accessible for young learners. The illustrations are evocative and deeply worthy of close reading and provide students access to describe "I Am," "I Can," "I Did" statements about the characters.

INVITATION 7
Hmm . . . Yes, And; Yes, But; No, Because

This invitation is designed to help students grow in their perspective-taking approaches while also learning how to respectfully engage as speakers and listeners. We know we feel valued when others truly listen to what we have to say and when they respond in a way that shows that they were listening (not just waiting for their turn to speak).

WARM UP: *Invite students to think about all the kinds of conversations in their life (in the classroom, on the playground, at home).*

Every day, we do a lot of listening and speaking to one another. You are having all kinds of conversations here in our classroom, out on the playground, and at home. One of the ways you can make someone else happy is by showing others that you are listening and by responding to what they said in a respectful way that adds on to their thinking.

TEACH: *Model ways to respond to someone respectfully by using the sentence starters "Yes, and"; "Yes, but"; and "No, because."*

Today, we are going to try three different ways to add on to what someone else has said by saying, "Yes, and" to add on to what the person said; "Yes, but" to acknowledge what they said but to disagree; and "No, because" to disagree and explain more about why.

TRY: *Invite students to have a quick conversation about a particular moment in a read-aloud.*

This seems like a page where we could have a lot to say about how the characters might feel at this moment. Turn and talk to a partner about how you think one of the characters feels right now. Remember, if you are the second speaker to try to use "Yes, and," "Yes, but," or "No, because" to show that you are listening but that you also have something to say.

CLARIFY: *Remind students that these sentence frames help us say more and to speak respectfully with one another even when we do not agree.*

When we have conversations with each other in class, these are helpful ways to respond to someone else. Challenge yourself today to use one of these sentence starters when having a conversation today out on the playground or when you are back at home. I'd love to hear about when you use them and what happens.

TEACHER TIPS

One of the factors that makes learning stick is repeated practice. For students to get comfortable using specific language to signal they are listening to someone else and to be able to add on or offer a counter-viewpoint takes intentional practice over time. Consider incorporating this invitation at different times in the year when you want students to respectfully listen but also say something. This invitation also works well before students engage in debates about nonfiction topics or before engaging in partner work.

LITERATURE SUGGESTIONS

One of my favorite books is Caldecott-winning *Wolf in the Snow* by Matthew Cordell (2017). Cordell thoughtfully counters stories we know about big, bad wolves, by offering readers a story where a little girl dressed in a red hooded jacket helps a wolf pup and is, in turn, helped by the wolf pack. Every page offers us something to say about whether the girl is making the right decision, and Cordell positions us to imagine what we would do in the girl's situation. For invitations like this one, I prefer to start by using wordless picture books that give students access to say something about what they see across the pages.

INVITATION 8
Three Good Things

In the book *Extra Yarn* written by Mac Barnett (2012) and illustrated by Jon Klassen, a young girl and a seemingly ordinary box of yarn transform a gray and bleak town into a place of hope and inspiration. When Annabelle stumbles upon a box of colorful yarn, she does the natural thing and starts knitting herself a sweater, and she finds that there is still extra yarn. The refrain of extra yarn carries the story as Annabelle knits yarn creations for the people in her community, particularly those that express negative feelings about her and her yarn. Inventive and inspiring, *Extra Yarn* helps readers reimagine the ways they can turn the negativity around us into something positive and hopeful. Annabelle is inherently grateful, giving, and generous. Use this or any of the literature suggestions as a way to launch a series of read-alouds about seeing the good.

WARM UP: *Invite students to think of something good that happened in their day so far. You may want to launch this lesson with a read-aloud from a book where a character emphasizes the power of positive thinking, such as* Extra Yarn *by Mac Barnett or one of the following suggestions in which children serve as beacons of hope.*

Every day we experience good things. Think to yourself for a moment about something good that has happened in your day.

TEACH: *Model through a think-aloud your own thoughts about three good things from your day.*

Did you know that thinking about three good things that happened in your day is a way to actually make yourself happier? So far in my day, the three things that have stood out to me that are good things from my day are: (name three good things from your day—perhaps something about how your students made you smile, something about feelings of gratitude extended from others, or something small that taps into our senses like a smell or taste that students can relate to).

TRY: *Invite students to turn and talk to a neighbor about their thinking.*

> *When you have an idea of something good that has happened in your day, turn and talk to a neighbor about what you are thinking.* Give students a few moments and then invite them through shared or interactive writing to share their thinking for a class anchor chart. Invite students to share what they notice about their collective "good things."

CLARIFY: *Remind students that even when we have tough moments in our day, we can always look for the good.*

> *We will all experience things that don't go our way or have occasional feelings of doubt. One thing you can always do for yourself is to try to move on from negative feelings by thinking of three good things that have happened in your day so far.*

TEACHER TIPS

Consider using this invitation when you see students deflated by something in their learning or when you notice things are challenging for students either as learners or in their social dynamics. Link this lesson to the practice of the five-minute journaling. Extend this lesson by noticing the ways characters across stories seem to focus on the good in their lives, and use that positive energy to enact change. You can do this with students by thinking about the three good things from a character's day even when they are unstated in the text. This is a direct way to have students draw inferences by using what they know from the story and from their own lives to draw a conclusion about what the character might say were three good things from their day.

If students have a difficult time thinking of good things from their day, you can help redirect their thinking by focusing on good things to come with a sentence starter like: "It's a good day for _____." This phrasing is used in the picture book *Ocean Meets Sky* by Terry and Eric Fan (2018).

LITERATURE SUGGESTIONS

Many recently released works of children's literature focus on the power of seeing the good including: *Extra Yarn* by Mac Barnett (2012), *Maybe Something Beautiful* by Isabel Campoy (2016), *Tiny, Perfect Things* by M.H. Clark (2018), *Hey, Wall: A Story of Art and Community* by Susan Verde (2018), and *Ocean Meets Sky* by Terry and Eric Fan (2018).

INVITATION 9
Asking Questions Gets Us to Better Questions

Why do some songs make you happy and others make you sad? Why don't trees ever talk? How deep does the sun go when it sinks into the sea? These are the quixotic questions that a philosophical fox named Marco is suddenly filled with when an antlered ship arrives in his hometown (Slater 2017). A model for asking questions, Marco is a character that ultimately wants to know the most important question he's struck upon: What's the best way to find a friend you can talk to?

Asking questions is part of living a life of inquiry. When we have the courage to ask questions, we feel compelled to ask more questions. Asking questions helps us ask better questions. We know from literacy research that questioning is not only a life skill but an important literacy skill as well. As readers, when we ask questions, we are activating our thinking and going deeper into a story. As writers, when we ask questions, we strengthen our work and the work of our peers from a place of genuine curiosity.

Use this invitation as a way to launch a Wonder Wall, which can become a space in your classroom for students to ask any and all questions they are wondering about at moments when the wondering strikes them. You may want to have a tactile way for students to create a chain of wonderings that can visually show how their questions are related.

WARM UP: *Invite students to notice the Wonder Wall display you have created.*

Today, we have something new in our classroom. What is here today for the first time?

TEACH: *Model your own question process about something you are wondering about by asking more than one related question.*

When we ask questions, we activate our thinking. And the more we ask questions, the better our questions become. I've been thinking lately about some big questions, and by using question words I was able to generate several related questions, all about the same thing, that helped me get to the most important question for me right now. (Have an anchor chart available to make question words accessible for students: *Who*? *What*? *Where*? *When*? *Why*? *How*? Also have potential question topics available like: friendships, family, hobbies, sports, the world, people, characters . . .)

TRY: *Invite students to jot down a wondering in the form of a question or to draw something they are wondering about. If they are ready, invite them to hang their wonderings on the Wonder Wall.*

What is something you are wondering about in your own life? You can use our anchor charts and my example to help you get started. Once you have one question, see if you can keep going with another related question. You may want to try another question word (like Marco did in The Antlered Ship*).*

CLARIFY: *Remind students that asking questions gets us to better questions.*

Our Wonder Wall is going to be a place full of our questions. When we ask one question, we can keep going with our thinking to ask another related question. That can help us get to the most important question we really want to ask.

TEACHER TIPS

Asking anyone to name a question they are thinking about can be difficult for the responder in that moment. Literature helps us have models for asking questions and, in turn, helps us generate our own questions with greater ease. Consider using *The Antlered Ship* or any of the following literature suggestions before asking students to generate their own questions. A good goal for students to have is to ask five related questions by going deeper. They can vary their question words or keep going with the question word *why* to keep narrowing down their thinking. This is not only important for critical inquiry but is an important step researchers often take before landing on a project idea.

LITERATURE SUGGESTIONS

Books that help model questioning tend to be full of characters that are philosophical in nature. Think about the philosophical wonderings Frog and Toad have in

Arnold Lobel's classic series or that the characters in Leo Leonni's stories have that serve as models for our own lives. The characters in these stories are always thinking and wondering about big ideas like how to be a better friend, how to show willpower when it's hard to do so, how to pay attention to nature and the world around us, and how to make ourselves and those around us happier. Other books that help students ask questions include: *Ideas Are All Around* by Philip Stead (2016), *Ocean Meets Sky* by Terry and Eric Fan (2018), *Why Am I Me?* by Paige Britt (2017), *On a Beam of Light: A Story of Albert Einstein* by Jennifer Berne (2013), as well as the trilogy *What Do You Do with an Idea? What Do You Do with a Problem?* and *What Do You Do with a Chance?* by Kobi Yamada (2014, 2016, 2018).

Wordless (and nearly wordless) picture books are also natural pathways for questioning because we have to wonder what the characters are thinking and feeling. Books like *Journey*, *Quest*, and *Return* by Aaron Becker (2013, 2014, 2016), *Imagine!* by Raúl Colón (2018), *Wolf in the Snow* by Matthew Cordell (2017), *Before Morning* by Joyce Sidman (2016), *Wait* by Antoinette Portis (2015), and *Here I Am* by Patti Kim (2015).

INVITATION 10
Listening with Love

What do we do when someone around us experiences something hard or even devastating? What strategies can we use to let someone know we are here and we are listening? Do we talk, offer solutions, help to rebuild, get angry, try to remember, laugh, hide, and pretend nothing happened? Or do we do more by simply being present for someone else? Spare and poignant, *The Rabbit Listened* by Cori Doerrfeld (2018) gives us some answers. Learning to listen is one of the hardest skills over our lifetime. As humans, we have the tendency to wait for our turn to speak. We have the tendency to want to fix the problems of others. But, there is a better way, and it's through listening with love.

This invitation is designed to help students consider their own tendencies when listening and to get stronger at listening by simply being present and sometimes waiting.

WARM UP: *Invite students to think of all the ways they can show someone else love.*

We are so fortunate in life to have people we love. Let's think about all of the ways we can show someone else that we love them. (Start a chart, possibly in the shape of a heart, to list student definitions and examples of what love is.)

TEACH: *Model for students what we can do to really listen to someone else.*

One of the most important ways I know someone loves me is when they really listen. But listening to someone else is really, really hard to do. Sometimes I want to jump in and just share my idea. Sometimes, I am thinking about something else when someone is talking. But sometimes, I do my best listening by simply being there for my friend. (Read aloud *The Rabbit Listened* as a way to grow students' thinking about how to help others when something goes wrong in someone else's life.)

TRY: *Invite students to notice and name ways we can grow as listeners.* (If you are using The Rabbit Listened, *consider having students act out different animals from the story. If you are not using this book, you can also have students act out ways to show they are listening or not listening to someone else.)*

> *Let's think about how we can show others we are listening. How can our bodies and our voices let others know we are listening? Turn and talk to a neighbor to share some ideas.*

CLARIFY: *Remind students that listening is a way to show love.*

> *When we really listen to someone else, we show that we care about what they are saying and that we care about them. Today and every day, challenge yourself to show someone else that you are listening.*

TEACHER TIPS

Use today as a springboard to more conversations about active listening. We show active listening by being fully present. That means looking in someone's eyes, nodding, using little words like *Hmm* and *Tell me more*. Consider making listening with love a class goal and record in a public place the stories students tell you about times that they listened to someone else or they felt they were really listened to.

Also consider extending the lesson to have students create a Love Gallery with different illustrations and expressions of love. What does love look like, sound like, feel like?

LITERATURE SUGGESTIONS

Listening is a skill that can grow in anyone. Some of us are more comfortable speaking and fill silence with words. Some of us are more comfortable deferring to others because we need more time to process our ideas or because we have been accustomed to listening before speaking. *The Rabbit Listened* by Cori Doerrfeld (2018) is a profound, yet simple story about the power of listening. Other books that explore listening and other ways to show love are: *Love* by Matt de la Peña (2018), *I Am Loved* by Nikki Giovanni (2018), *Waiting* by Kevin Henkes (2015), *Corduroy* by Don Freeman (1968), and *And Tango Makes Three* by Justin Richardson and Peter Parnell (2005).

Part 3

APPENDICES

Conversation Prompts to Get to Know Students and What Makes Them Happy

What is a time you remember where someone did something really kind for you?

If you could have any magic ability, what would it be, and how would you use it?

What is something you love about yourself? What is something you think your friends and family love about you? Tell me more.

What is a time when you remember being really happy (excited, nervous, upset, frustrated)? Imagine that time in your mind, and tell me about it. Who was with you, and what happened?

What is a hero? Who is your hero? How can you be a hero?

Whose smile brings you the most joy?

What are some of the things you are most proud of yourself for? Tell me more about why.

What are some things you like to do alone? Why?

What's a smell that reminds you of home? Tell me about that.

Talk about a time you tried something new.

What is a time you remember doing something kind for someone else? What happened?

What are some things you like to do with other people? Why?

If you could change something about the world, what would it be?

Who are your "laugh buddies" or people you laugh with a lot? Tell me about something that made you laugh together.

190

What is one thing adults do not understand?

Have you conquered a fear? If so, how?

What is something you love about where you live? Tell me more about that.

What is the most courageous thing you have seen somebody do?

What's an object that holds special meaning to you? Why?

What do you think makes someone a true friend? How do you know? Tell me more about your friends and things you do together.

APPENDIX B
Lesson-Planning Tool to Design for Happiness

Although lesson plan designs will vary, most research-based instruction will include a warm-up in the beginning to grab student attention, purposeful modeling, opportunities for students to actively engage or try, more extended independent practice, and a wrap-up to provide closure. The following are suggestions for strategic moments in your lesson to intentionally design for student happiness. Think about which of these suggestions you are already embedding in your instruction and where you can try to be more intentional in your planning to boost student happiness.

Warm Up: Build student interest. Foster connection to the text, the topic, and each other. Invite students to discover something new in this lesson. Use playful language where possible. Use a story to grab student attention.

Teach: Model your own discovery process as a learner.

Try: Invite students to try by framing learning as a worthwhile challenge. Incorporate movement if possible through gestures and small actions.

Clarify: Remind students of the teaching point; again encourage feelings of discovery and frame learning as a worthwhile challenge.

Independent Practice: Provide students with some level of choice as learners to be self-driven in their decision making.

Wrap Up: Invite students to share how they grew as learners today: What choices did they make? What did they discover through reading or writing? What did they discover about themselves? What connections did they make to the text or each other? What challenges did they face and how did they solve them?

APPENDIX C
Lesson-Planning Template to Design for Happiness

This lesson includes:

☐ Connection   ☐ Choice   ☐ Challenge

☐ Play   ☐ Story   ☐ Discovery

☐ Movement

Warm Up Did you ever . . . ? Let me tell you a story about . . .	
Teach Watch me as I try and discover . . .	
Try Because _____, you are ready to _____. (Turn and talk to a neighbor, show on your face _____, point to _____, jot ____.)	
Clarify What will you discover today? Remember that . . .	
Independent Practice Think about the choices you are making today . . .	
Wrap Up Your best is always enough. We are excited to hear your voices and to learn about your choices. What did you discover through reading or writing today? What did you discover about yourself? What connections did you make? What challenges did you face, and how did you solve them?	

APPENDIX D
Story Frames to Launch a Year of Happiness

BEST PART OF ME

Use with Wendy Ewald's book *The Best Part of Me* (2002) to provide mentor texts for students by students.

Think about the things you love most about yourself that you want others to know.

Start by listing all the things you love about yourself.

Then, put a star next to the thing you most love about yourself that you want others to know.

Next, make a list of all the reasons why you love that about yourself.

Finally, through writing and drawing explain to others what you love most about yourself and why.

I love about myself:

Why I love that about myself:

WHERE I'M FROM

Use with George Ella Lyon's poem "Where I'm From" (1999) as a mentor text.

Where we are from is a part of our story. We are from the people we love, the places we live, and the memories we have.

Think about what you love about where you live. Draw a map of your neighborhood or home with all the places you love. If you want, add the people you love and how they connect to where you live.

Next, imagine you are describing where you are from to someone else who has never been there before. To help you, share your ideas about the following questions with someone else:

Who are the people you love there, and what makes them special to you?

What are the things you see?

What are the things you smell?

What are the foods you taste?

What do you hear people saying a lot?

What are other sounds you hear?

What are family or neighborhood traditions you have?

What are objects or parts of nature that make where you are from special?

Writing Extensions
(to keep writing about where you are from)

Write about a smell that reminds you of home. What is it? Take us back to a time you were home and experienced that smell.

Write about a sound that reminds you of home. What is it? Take us back to a time you were home and heard that sound.

Write about a taste that reminds you of home. What is it? Take us back to a time you were home and tasted that!

Write about something you see out your window at home. What is it? Describe what you see.

Write about a beloved object that reminds you of home. What is it? Describe what it looks like and why it's important to you.

WHO I LOVE

Some of the best stories remind us that loving others is one of the best things about life. Every great character has someone that helps them along the way.

Writing from Your Life

First, list all the people you love with a little note about why you love them.

Then, pick one person to focus on.

Tell a story about a time when you and that person did something together.
- Who was with you?
- Where were you?
- What were you doing together?
- What were you thinking to yourself?
- What do you think you said to each other?
- How did you feel? Imagine what your facial expression was to show that feeling.

Writing from Your Imagination

Create two characters that love each other but might seem like unlikely friends. It could be two family members or two friends. What is an adventure they can have together where their friendship is tested in some way? Think about characters you know that are best friends (like Frog and Toad, Elephant and Piggie, or television characters that are best friends like the Kratt Brothers in *Wild Kratts*) and what they do together.

Create two characters that are going to be friends.

What are they each like?

What is something they can do together?

Does one of the characters have a problem that the other can help solve?

What can they think to themselves as the story unfolds?

What do you think they could say to each other?

How do they feel? Imagine what their facial expression looks like to show those feelings.

WHAT IF

A lot of great stories start out by asking "what if" questions that no one else had ever asked.

Writing from Your Imagination

Start by listing as many "what if" questions that you can think of like:

- What if I could go back in time?
- What if I had magical powers?
- What if animals could talk?
- What if toys had feelings?

Choose your favorite "what if" question and create a main character that can experience this adventure. Is it you? Is it a make-believe character? Draw who it will be.

How will your character feel? (scared, alone, nervous, proud, left out, ambitious, unsure, brave)

Who are helpers who can help them navigate those feelings to experience some kind of change?

Writing to Make a Better World

Start by listing as many "what if" questions that you can think of like:

- What if there were no wars?
- What if everyone had enough food to eat?
- What if everyone was loved?

Choose your favorite "what if" question and write about why this is an important topic to you.

WHEN I CHANGED

We all have times in life where we feel changed.

Change can happen when we experience firsts, like doing something on your own for the first time—riding a subway, walking home, making dinner, or caring for a sibling.

We also feel changed when we realize we are getting stronger at something because we worked hard—running a longer distance, learning a new language, reading a new book.

We also feel changed thanks to the kindness of others—someone made us realize how special we are or makes a difference in our life.

Writing from Your Life

Think about a time when you felt changed. What happened to make you act, think, or feel differently? Draw and write about that moment when you realized you were changed and what led up to that change.

Writing from Your Imagination

Think about an imaginary character who can experience some kind of change. Who do you want your character to be? How do you want them to change?

- Do you want your character to do something for the first time?
- Do you want your character to get stronger at something?
- Do you want your character to change thanks to others?

WHO WILL I BE?

We all have hopes and dreams. To make our dreams a reality, we have to imagine ourselves living that dream.

Writing from Your Life

Think about the people you admire most and why you admire them. Who do you want to be like? Why?

Draw and write about them.

Or

When you picture yourself as a grown-up, what do you want to be doing? Why?

Start by making your dream map. This is a drawing of all the dreams you have for yourself.

Then, pick one dream and draw and write about how you see yourself living that dream in the future.

APPENDIX E
Five-Minute Journaling Prompt Ideas

Five-minute journaling prompts are based on the science of happiness. When established as a routine, this daily journaling has the power to shape thoughts, change mindsets, and impact actions. There are many different ways to incorporate five-minute journaling into your classroom routine. Find the way that works for you and your students.

You can:

- Use blank notebooks and glue the prompts to the front cover as an invitation for students to journal about any of the prompts.
- Use blank notebooks and glue the prompts to the front cover and have students respond to all of the prompts if they can that day.
- Have students make covers that reflect their personalities, hopes, or dreams.
- Model with your own journal.
- Incorporate blank pages for other kinds of writing/drawing.

Morning

I am grateful for . . .

I am looking forward to . . .

I am . . .

Afternoon

Something amazing that happened today . . .

I could have made today better by _____

I learned today . . .

I made someone else happy by . . .

APPENDIX F
Designing Physical Spaces to Foster Happiness

What do space and furniture have to do with student engagement, learning, and happiness? Our bodies and minds respond to the spaces we spend time in. We are also physical and social creatures. Our classroms are spaces that are homes away from home. They can be spaces that activate all of the senses and intentionally uplift students. Teaching in New York City, some years my classrooms were tiny spaces and I didn't have a budget for extras. Some of the ideas in this section may feel possible, and others may seem aspirational. The physical design choices you make will need to reflect the number of students in your care and the existing furniture, shelving, wall space, and windows. Think of these ideas as food for thought.

Space for Movement

One of the most overlooked sites of possibility for student happiness is providing enough space for students to engage in movement when they need to. In Lina's first-grade classroom, movement is a key priority right from the start of the day. Her students put their belongings in their lockers, and then each day they walk into the classroom and choose where they are going to sit for the day. Yes, these six- and seven-year-olds are empowered to choose which table they will sit at, what kind of chair they will sit in, and who they will be sitting with that day. There is no assigned seating, and students make choices that work for them every single day. Students are also not required to sit or stand in any particular way. Rather, they are invited to make their own choices. In Lina's classroom, space is maximized for collaboration, but there is also space for students to self-select a quieter or more independent work station. When they need to move, they do so, and because it is an invitation to everyone when they need it, students understand why others are moving and it does not become a distraction.

Student materials are also located strategically so that students have reasons to get up to find a new sheet of paper from a variety of choices, or to book shop, or to consult an anchor chart as a resource for their own learning.

Thanks to grants, Lina's students also have access to a variety of seats that provide movement from wobbly stools to rocking buckets. Even sitting itself has options for movement.

© 2019 by Katie Egan Cunningham from *Start with Joy*. Portsmouth, NH: Stenhouse. May be photocopied for classroom use only

- In your classroom, what routines can foster students to make choices about times when they need movement, and what options can students have to move around the classroom with purpose and intentionality?
- Are student materials located in areas of the classroom that invite movement by design?
- Are learning resources like anchor charts hung in strategic locations so that students can be invited to get up and consult a resource when they need to?

Space for Connection

Although student happiness can be boosted through simple, intentional designs in physical space to allow for movement, our classroom spaces can also be designed for connection. One of the most valuable spaces in any classroom are places for students to simply connect, talk, and tap into their inner social being. Although you may have your students seated in tables to foster connection, there is also value in having a designated classroom area for connections beyond who is sitting at your table. In Lina's classroom, she has a low table with a plush campfire in the center that serves as a reference for students to imagine they are sitting by a fire having a chat. Sometimes this area is used for small-group instruction, but other times it's a choice area for students to go when they want to talk to someone about what they are reading or when they feel ready to confer with a writing partner. Sometimes it is simply a space for students to gather during choice time, not to build or draw or write but just to chat. Lina has honored the social selves of her students through this special area designed with connection in mind.

- In your classroom, what are the possibilities for spaces for students to connect as readers, but also as young people?
- If you have students seated at tables, do they have some ownership over who they sit with? Can they?
- Are there possibilities for fostering further connections by partnering with another class for special projects but also for choice time so that students have more possibilities for connection?

Space for Growing Independence

Although connection is critical to our happiness and the happiness of our students, it is also important that our classroom spaces provide opportunities for students to grow in their independence as readers, writers, and creators. Classroom libraries can be designed for students to access books they want to read and that they feel they have the strategies to be able to successfully navigate. Although it may be a messy process, redesigning your classroom library to be organized by genre, series, author, and topic and by student suggestion is a critically worthwhile process that can nearly instantly boost student agency and ownership over their reading.

In addition to classroom library design, you can also design other classroom spaces with independence in mind. Rather than limit students to particular paper formats, have a paper choice area designated for students to choose the paper that will best work for them as writers and creators. Include in this area a variety of illustration materials such as colored pencils, crayons, cray-pas, watercolors, scraps of paper, glue, scissors, and hole punches.

Your wall space can serve as another teacher in the room. What you hang, where you hang it, and why you are hanging it can be explained to students so that they know they are invited to access helpful information when they need it. Our eyes tend to seek out particular colors, so consider the color choices you make on your anchor charts so that particular words pop out for students. Also consider having a color scheme across your charts so that students' eyes are not inundated with too many colors or too much information.

You may have a word wall in your classroom to help students quickly access important words including classmates' names, high-frequency words, and words that break phonetic rules. Make sure that the words are written or typed in a font that replicates the formation of letters (notice the *a*, for example—Century Gothic has an *a* that is much more student friendly than Times New Roman or Arial: ɑ). Sit where your students sit and notice whether you can easily read the words on the word wall. Usually words need to be in much bigger print than I typically see in classroom word walls for students to quickly and easily access the words either from their seat or by going up to the wall.

Finally, is there a space in the classroom where students can choose to go (think invitation not punishment) if they want a quiet area to work or concentrate. Even the most social students need time to quietly process and think. It's helpful if it is a space set off from table chatter and if there are resources available to consult for letters and letter formation, a mini word wall with words already taught, and even an inspiring message for students to know that their best is always enough.

APPENDIX G
Media Recommendations

Some of our best resources as teachers to energize and engage our students come from thoughtful media productions. Thanks to YouTube, many video clips can be easily accessed and incorporated into lessons as part of your warm up. Although not time-consuming, these media recommendations (largely from Pixar films) add sparks of joy, laughter, and excitement that also come from great storytelling. The creators of these media suggestions are masters of their craft, and this list will only grow as high-quality media for children continues to be produce

Brave
youtube.com/watch?v=2EIFWjLYNWA
What's in a character's heart?
What can characters teach us?

Up
youtube.com/watch?v=XubM62q9nlw
How can we compare characters?
What advice can we give characters on how they treat each other?

The Present (this short animation has won nearly sixty awards, and the animators were immediately given positions at Disney)
https://vimeo.com/152985022
What emotions are characters feeling (need to see the full three minutes to get to this)?
How do the ways a character changes help us think about our own lives?
How do a character's struggles help us better understand a story and ourselves?
How does understanding a character's motivation help us understand what we would/could do in a similar situation?

Despicable Me
youtube.com/watch?v=Xmmx93odvdo
What emotions are characters feeling (need to see the full three minutes to get to this)?
How do the ways a character changes help us think about our own lives?

How do a character's struggles help us better understand a story and ourselves?

How does understanding a character's motivation help us understand what we would/could do in a similar situation?

Big Hero Six

youtube.com/watch?v=SRHU4264Xwc

What emotions are characters feeling (need to see the full three minutes to get to this)?

How do the ways a character changes help us think about our own lives?

How do a character's struggles help us better understand a story and ourselves?

How does understanding a character's motivation help us understand what we would/could do in a similar situation?

REFERENCES

CHILDREN'S LITERATURE

Abouraya, Karen L. 2019. *Malala Yousafzai: Warrior with Words*. New York: Scholastic.

Ahmed, Road. 2018. *Mae Among the Stars*. New York: HarperCollins.

Alexander, Kwame. 2014. *The Crossover*. Boston: Houghton Mifflin Harcourt.

Andrews, Troy. 2015. *Trombone Shorty*. New York: Scholastic.

Applegate, Katherine. 2017. *Wishtree*. New York: Feiwel and Friends.

Armand, Glenda. 2015. *Ira's Shakespeare Dream*. New York: Lee and Low Books.

Arnold, Tedd. 2005. *Hi! Fly Guy*. New York: Scholastic.

Baker, Jeannie. 2010. *Mirror*. Somerville, MA: Candlewick.

Barnett, Mac. 2012. *Extra Yarn*. Somerville, MA: Candlewick.

———. 2017. *Triangle*. Somerville, MA: Candlewick.

———. 2017. *The Wolf, the Duck, and the Mouse*. Somerville, MA: Candlewick.

———. 2018. *Square*. Somerville, MA: Candlewick.

Beaty, Andrea. 2007. *Iggy Peck, Architect*. New York: Abrams Books for Young Readers.

———. 2013. *Rosie Revere, Engineer*. New York: Abrams Books for Young Readers.

Becker, Aaron. 2013. *Journey*. Somerville, MA: Candlewick.

———. 2014. *Quest*. Somerville, MA: Candlewick.

———. 2016. *Return*. Somerville, MA: Candlewick.

Berne, Jennifer. 2013. *On a Beam of Light: A Story of Albert Einstein*. San Francisco: Chronicle Books.

Boelts, Maribeth. 2009. *Those Shoes*. Somerville, MA: Candlewick.

Bridges, Shirin Yim. 2002. *Ruby's Wish*. San Francisco: Chronicle Books.

Briggs, Raymond. 1978. *The Snowman*. New York: Random House Books for Young Readers.

Britt, Paige. 2017. *Why Am I Me?* New York: Scholastic.

Buyea, Rob. 2011. *Because of Mr. Terupt*. New York: Yearling.

Byers, Grace. 2018. *I Am Enough*. New York: Balzer and Bray.

Campbell, K. G. 2014. *The Mermaid and the Shoe*. Toronto: Kids Can Press.

Campoy, Isabel. 2016. *Maybe Something Beautiful: How Art Transformed a Neighborhood*. Boston: Houghton Mifflin Harcourt.

Carle, Eric. 2011. *The Artist Who Painted a Blue Horse*. New York: Philomel Books.

Clark, M. H. 2018. *Tiny, Perfect Things*. Seattle, WA: Compendium.

Cole, Henry. 2012. *Unspoken: A Story from the Underground Railroad*. New York: Scholastic.

Cole, Joanna. 1986. *The Magic School Bus at the Waterworks*. New York: Scholastic.

Colón, Raúl. 2018. *Imagine!* New York: Simon and Schuster.

Cordell, Matthew. 2017. *Wolf in the Snow*. New York: Feiwel and Friends.

Cornwall, Gaia. 2017. *Jabari Jumps*. Somerville, MA: Candlewick.

Dahl, Roald. 1964. *Charlie and the Chocolate Factory*. New York: Alfred A. Knopf.

———. 1988. *Matilda*. New York: Alfred A. Knopf.

Daywalt, Drew. 2013. *The Day the Crayons Quit*. New York: Philomel Books.

de Arias, Patricia. 2018. *Marwan's Journey*. Kooloon Bay, Hong Kong: Minedition.

de la Peña, Matt. 2015. *Last Stop on Market Street*. New York: G.P. Putnam's Sons Books for Young Readers.

———. 2018. *Love*. New York: G.P.Putnam's Sons Books for Young Readers.

Docter, Pete, and Ronnie Del Carmen. 2015. Inside Out. Emeryville, CA: Pixar Animation Studios, Walt Disney Pictures.

Doerrfeld, Cori. 2018. *The Rabbit Listened*. New York: Dial Books.

Dr. Seuss. 1957. *How the Grinch Stole Christmas*. New York: Random House.

Ellis, Deborah. 2000. *The Breadwinner*. Toronto, Canada: Groundwood Books.

Engle, Margarita. 2015. *Drum Dream Girl*. Boston, MA: Houghton Mifflin Harcourt Books for Young Readers.

Ewald, Wendy. 2002. *The Best Part of Me: Children Talk About Their Bodies in Pictures and Words*. New York: Little, Brown Books for Young Readers.

Fan, Terry, and Eric Fan. 2018. *Ocean Meets Sky*. New York: Simon and Schuster Books for Young Readers.

Floca, Brian. 2013. *Locomotive*. New York: Atheneum Books for Young Readers.

Fox, Mem. 1997. *Whoever You Are*. Boston, MA: Houghton Mifflin Harcourt Children's Books.

Freeman, Don. 1968. *Corduroy*. New York: Viking Books for Young Readers.

Giovanni, Nikki. 2018. *I Am Loved*. New York: Atheneum.

Goeminne, S. 2017. *No One Else Like You*. Louisville, KY: Westminster John Knox.

Golding, William. 1954. *Lord of the Flies*. London: Faber and Faber.

Goodman, Susan. 2016. *The First Step: How One Girl Put Segregation on Trial*. New York: Bloomsbury Children's.

Hall, Michael. 2015. *Red: A Crayon's Story*. New York: Greenwillow Books.

Harrison, Vashti. 2017. *Little Leaders: Bold Women in Black History*. New York: Little, Brown Books for Young Readers.

Henkes, Kevin. 2015. *Waiting*. New York: Greenwillow Books.

Holub, Joan. 2016. *Little Red Writing*. San Francisco: Chronicle Books.

Hong, Jess. 2017. *Lovely*. Berkeley, CA: Creston Books.

Hood, Susan. 2018. *Shaking Things Up: 14 Young Women Who Changed the World*. New York: HarperCollins.

hooks, bell. 2004. *Skin Again*. New York: Jump At the Sun.

Hopkinton, Deborah. 2016. *Steamboat School: Inspired by a True Story*. New York: Disney-Hyperion.

House, Silas, and Neela Vaswani. 2012. *Same Sun Here*. Somerville, MA: Candlewick.

Idle, Molly. 2013. *Flora and the Flamingo*. San Francisco, CA: Chronicle Books.

Jacques, Brian. 1986. *Redwall*. New York: Penguin Random House.

Jeffers, Oliver. 2005. *Lost and Found*. New York: Philomel Books.

———. 2011. *Stuck*. New York: Philomel Books.

Jordan, Deloris, and Roslyn M. Jordan. 2000. *Salt in His Shoes: Michael Jordan in Pursuit of a Dream*. New York: Simon and Schuster Books for Young Readers.

Judge, Lita. 2011. *Red Sled*. New York: Atheneum Books for Young Readers.

Jullien, Jean. 2016. *This Is Not a Book*. New York: Phaidon.

Katz, Karen. 2002. *The Colors of Us*. New York: Square Fish.

Keats, Ezra Jack. 1964. *Whistle for Willie*. New York: Viking.

Kelly, Shelley. 2009. *Shades of People*. New York: Holiday House.

Kelsey, Elin. 2015. *Wild Ideas: Let Nature Inspire Your Thinking*. Toronto, Canada: Owlkids.

Kim, Patti. 2015. *Here I Am*. Mankato, MN: Picture Window Books.

Kinney, Jeff. 2007. *Diary of a Wimpy Kid*. New York: Amulet Books.

Klassen, Jon. 2011. *I Want My Hat Back*. Somerville, MA: Candlewick.

———. 2012. *This Is Not My Hat*. Somerville, MA: Candlewick.

———. 2016. *We Found a Hat*. Somerville, MA: Candlewick.

Kostecki-Shaw, Jenny Sue. 2011. *Same, Same but Different*. New York: Henry Holt.

Kuhlmann, Torben. 2016. *Armstrong: The Adventurous Journey of a Mouse to the Moon*. New York: NorthSouth Books.

Lamarche, Jim. 2000. *The Raft*. New York: HarperCollins.

Lawson, Jon Arno. 2015. *Sidewalk Flowers*. Toronto, Canada: Groundwood Books.

Leannah, Michael. 2017. *Most People*. Thomaston, ME: Tilbury House Publishers.

Lee, Suzy. 2017. *Lines*. San Francisco: Chronicle Books.

Lehman, Barbara. 2004. *The Red Book*. Boston: Houghton Mifflin Harcourt Books for Young Readers.

Leonni, Leo. 1967. *Frederick*. New York: Pantheon Books.

Lester, Jules. 2008. *Let's Talk About Race*. New York: HarperCollins.

Lewis, C. S. 1950. *The Lion, the Witch, and the Wardrobe*. London: Geoffrey Bles.

Lobel, Arnold. 1970. *Frog and Toad Are Friends*. New York: HarperCollins.

———. 1972. *Frog and Toad Together*. New York: HarperCollins.

Ludwig, Trudy. 2013. *The Invisible Boy*. New York: Penguin Random House.

Luyken, Corinna. 2017. *The Book of Mistakes*. New York: Dial Books.

Markel, Michelle. 2013. *Brave Girl: Clara and the Shirtwaist Makers' Strike of 1909*. New York: Balzer and Bray.

Mattick, Lindsay. 2015. *Finding Winnie: The True Story of the World's Most Famous Bear*. Boston: Little, Brown.

Medina, Juana. 2016. *Juana and Lucas*. Somerville, MA: Candlewick.

Messner, Kate. 2011. *Over and Under the Snow*. San Francisco: Chronicle Books.

———. 2015. *Up in the Garden and Down in the Dirt*. San Francisco: Chronicle Books.

———. 2017. *Over and Under the Pond*. San Francisco: Chronicle Books.

Milne, Alan Alexander. 1928/1988. *The House at Pooh Corner*. New York: Dutton Books for Young Readers.

Mumford, James. 2010. *Rain School*. Boston: Houghton Mifflin Harcourt Books for Young Readers.

Munroe, Randall. 2015. *Thing Explainer: Complicated Stuff in Simple Words*. Boston: Houghton Mifflin Harcourt.

Munsch, Robert. 1980. *The Paperbag Princess*. Toronto: Annick.

Muth, Jon. 2002. *The Three Questions*. New York: Scholastic.

Myers, Christopher. 2000. *Wings*. New York: Scholastic.

Novak, B. J. 2014. *The Book With No Pictures*. New York: Dial Books.

Obama, Barack. 2010. *Of Thee I Sing: A Letter to My Daughters*. New York: Alfred A. Knopf.

Otoshi, Katherine. 2008. *One*. San Rafael, CA: KO Kids Books.

Palacio, R. J. 2012. *Wonder*. New York: Knopf Books for Young Readers.

———. 2017. *We're All Wonders*. New York: Knopf Books for Young Readers.

Parr, Todd. 2014. *It's Okay to Make Mistakes*. New York: Little, Brown Books for Young Readers.

Perkins, Lynne Rae. 2016. *Frank and Lucky Get Schooled*. New York: Greenwillow Books.

Pinkney, Jerry. 2009. *The Lion and the Mouse*. Boston: Little, Brown.

Pollack, Pam, and Meg Belviso. 2014. *Who Was Susan B. Anthony?* New York: Penguin.

Portis, Antoinette. 2015. *Wait*. New York: Roaring Brook Press.

Rashka, Chris. 2011. *A Ball for Daisy*. New York: Schwartz and Wade Books.

———. 2013. *Everyone Can Learn to Ride a Bicycle*. New York: Schwartz and Wade Books.

Rathman, Peggy. 2000. *Good Night, Gorilla*. New York: Puffin Books.

Reynolds, Peter. 2012. *Sky Color*. Somerville, MA: Candlewick.

———. 2018. *The Word Collector*. New York: Scholastic.

———. 2019. *Say Something*. New York: Scholastic.

Richardson, Justin, and Peter Parnell. 2005. *And Tango Makes Three*. New York: Simon and Schuster.

Rockliff, Mara. 2015. *Mesmerized: How Ben Franklin Solved a Mystery That Baffled All of France*. Somerville, MA: Candlewick.

Rowling, J. K. 1999. *Harry Potter and the Sorcerer's Stone*. New York: Scholastic.

Ruzzier, Sergio. 2018. *Fox and Chick: The Party and Other Stories*. San Francisco: Chronicle Books.

Ryan, Pam Muñoz. 2015. *Echo*. New York: Scholastic.

Rylant, Cynthia. 1996. *Henry and Mudge The First Book*. New York: Aladdin Paperbacks.

———. 1996. *Poppleton*. New York: Blue Sky Press.

Santat, Dan. 2014. *The Adventures of Beekle: The Unimaginary Friend*. Boston: Little, Brown.

———. 2014. *After the Fall: How Humpty Dumpty Got Back Up Again*. New York: Little, Brown.

———. 2016. *Are We There Yet?* New York: Little, Brown.

Shetterly, Margot Lee. 2018. *Hidden Figures: The True Story of Four Black Women and the Space Race*. New York: William Morrow and Company.

Sidman, Joyce. 2016. *Before Morning*. Boston: Houghton Mifflin Harcourt.

Silverstein, Shel. 2974. *Where the Sidewalk Ends*. New York: HarperCollins.

Simon, Seymour. 2003. *Earth*. New York: Simon & Schuster Books for Young Readers.

Slater, Dashka. 2017. *The Antlered Ship*. La Jolla, CA: Beach Lane Books.

Spinelli, Eileen. 2008. *The Best Story*. New York: Dial Books.

Spires, Ashley. 2014. *The Most Magnificent Thing*. Toronto: Kids Can Press.

———. 2017. *The Thing Lou Couldn't Do*. Toronto: Kids Can Press.

Stead, Philip. 2010. *A Sick Day for Amos McGee*. New York: Neal Porter Books.

———. 2012. *Bear Has a Story to Tell*. New York: Roaring Brook.

———. 2016. *Ideas Are All Around*. New York: Roaring Brook.

———. 2016. *Samson in the Snow*. New York: Roaring Brook.

Steptoe, Javaka. 2016. *Radiant Child: The Story of Young Artist Jean-Michel Basquiat*. New York: Little, Brown.

Thompson, Laurie Ann. 2015. *Emmanuel's Dream: The True Story of Emmanuel Ofosu Yeboah*. New York: Schwartz and Wade.

Tonatiah, Duncan. 2014. *Separate Is Never Equal: Sylvia Mendez and Her Family's Fight for Desegregation*. New York: Harry N. Abrams.

Trivizas, Eugene. 1997. *The Three Little Wolves and the Big Bad Pig*. Margaret K. McElderry Books.

Tullet, Hervé. 2017. *Say Zoop!* San Francisco: Chronicle Books.

Verde, Susan. 2015. *I Am Yoga*. New York: Harry N. Abrams.

———. 2017. *I Am Peace: A Book of Mindfulness*. New York: Harry N. Abrams.

———. 2018. *I Am Human: A Book of Empathy*. New York: Harry N. Abrams.

———. 2018. *Hey Wall: A Story of Art and Community*. New York: Simon and Schuster.

———. 2019. *I Am Love: A Book of Compassion*. New York: Harry N. Abrams.

Viorst, Judith. 1972. *Alexander and the Terrible, Horrible, No Good, Very Bad Day*. New York: Atheneum Books for Young Readers.

Weisner, David. 2006. *Flotsam*. New York: Clarion Books.

Wenzel, Brendan. 2016. *They All Saw a Cat*. San Francisco: Chronicle Books.

Willems, Mo. 2003. *Don't Let the Pigeon Drive the Bus*. New York: Disney-Hyperion.

———. 2004. *Knuffle Bunny: A Cautionary Tale*. New York: Hachette Books.

———. 2007. *My Friend Is Sad: An Elephant and Piggie Book.* New York: Disney-Hyperion.

———. 2011. *Should I Share My Ice Cream?: An Elephant and Piggie Book*. New York: Disney-Hyperion.

Yamada, Kobi. 2014. *What Do You Do with an Idea?* Seattle, WA: Compendium.

———. 2016. *What Do You Do with a Problem?* Seattle, WA: Compendium.

———. 2018. *What Do You Do with a Chance?* Seattle, WA: Compendium.

Yolen, Jane. 2016. *What to Do with a Box*. Mankato, MN: Creative Editions.

PROFESSIONAL WORKS

Achor, Shawn. 2018. *Big Potential: How Transforming the Pursuit of Success Raises Our Achievement, Happiness, and Well-Being.* Redfern, Australia: Currency.

Allington, Richard, and Rachael E. Gabriel. 2012. "Every Child, Every Day." *Educational Leadership* 69 (6): 10–15.

Allyn, Pam, and Ernest Morrell. 2016. *Every Child a Super Reader: 7 Strengths to Open a World of Possible.* New York: Scholastic.

Anderson, Mike. 2016. *Learning to Choose, Choosing to Learn: The Key to Student Motivation and Achievement.* Alexandria, VA: Association for Supervision and Curriculum Development.

Applegate, Anthony J., and Mary Dekonty Applegate. 2004. "The Peter Effect: Reading Habits and Attitudes of Preservice Teachers." *The Reading Teacher* 57: 554–563.

Atwell, Nancie. 2007. *The Reading Zone.* New York: Scholastic.

Bandura, Albert. 1986. *Social Foundations of Thought and Action: A Social Cognitive Theory.* Englewood Cliffs, NJ: Prentice Hall.

Barnes, Douglas R., and Frankie Todd. 1995. *Communication and Learning Revisited: Making Meaning Through Talk.* Portsmouth, NH: Heinemann.

Beilock, Sian. 2015. *How the Body Knows Its Mind: The Surprising Power of the Physical Environment to Influence How You Think and Feel.* New York: Atria Books.

Brackett, Marc. 2019. *Permission to Feel: Unlocking the Power of Emotions to Help Our Kids, Ourselves, and Our Society Thrive.* New York: Celadon Books.

Brooks, Jacqueline Grennon. 2004. "To See Beyond the Lesson." *Educational Leadership.* 62(1): 8-13.

Brown, Brené. 2017. *Braving the Wilderness: The Quest for True Belonging and the Courage to Stand Alone.* New York: Random House.

Browne, Stuart. 2010. *Play: How It Shapes the Brain, Opens the Imagination, and Invigorates the Soul.* New York: Avery.

Burkins, Jan, and Kim Yaris. 2016. *Who's Doing the Work?: How to Say Less So Readers Can Do More.* Portsmouth, NH: Stenhouse.

Cain, Susan. 2012. *Quiet: The Power of Introverts in a World That Can't Stop Talking.* New York: Broadway Books.

Calkins, Lucy M. 1986. *The Art of Teaching Writing*. Portsmouth, New Hampshire: Heinemann.

Chartock, Jonas, and Ross Wiener. 2014. "How to Save Teachers from Burning Out, Dropping Out, and Other Hazards of Experience." *The Hechinger Report*. Available online at: hechingerreport.org/content/can-keep-great-teachers-engaged-effective-settle-careers_18026.

Coiro, Julie. 2000. "Why Read Aloud?" *Early Childhood Today* 152: 12–14.

Csikszentmihalyi, Mihaly. 1990. *Flow: The Psychology of Optimal Experience*. New York: Harper and Row.

Cuddy, Amy. 2015. *Presence: Bringing Your Boldest Self to Your Biggest Challenges*. Boston: Little, Brown.

Data Resource Center for Child and Adolescent Health. 2016. "National Survey of Children's Health." childhealthdata.org/learn-about-the-nsch/NSCH.

Deci, Edward L. 1975. *Intrinsic Motivation*. New York: Plenum.

Deci, Edward L. and Richard M. Ryan. 1995. *Human Autonomy: The Basis for True Self-Esteem*. In M. Kemis (Ed.), *Efficacy, Agency, and Self-Esteem*: 31-49. New York: Plenum.

Despicable Me. 2010. Directed by Pierre Coffin and Chris Renaud. Screenplay by Cinco Paul and Ken Daurio. Based on a story by Sergio Pablos. Universal City, CA: Universal Studios Home Entertainment.

Doucleff, Michaeleen. 2018. "A Lost Secret: How to Get Kids to Pay Attention." *All Things Considered*. National Public Radio. Available online at: npr.org/sections/goatsandsoda/2018/06/21/621752789/a-lost-secret-how-to-get-kids-to-pay-attention.

Duckworth, Angela. 2016. *Grit: The Power of Passion and Perseverance*. New York: Scribner.

Duke, Nell, and Anne-Lise Halvorsen. 2017. "New Study Shows the Impact of Project Based Learning on Student Achievement." Edutopia: edutopia.org/article/new-study-shows-impact-pbl-student-achievement-nell-duke-anne-lise-halvorsen.

Durant, Will. 1926. *The Story of Philosophy: The Lives and Opinions of the World's Greatest Philosophers from Plato to John Dewey*. New York: Pocket Books.

Dweck, Carol. 2006. *Mindset: The New Pscyhology of Success*. New York: Penguin Random House.

Dyson, Anne Haas, and Celia Genishi. 1994. *The Need for Story: Cultural Diversity in Classroom and Community*. Urbana, IL: National Council of Teachers of English.

Elkind, David. 2007. *The Power of Play: How Spontaneous, Imaginative Activities Lead to Happier, Healthier Children*. Boston: De Capo Lifelong Books. Foundation for Art and Healing. "Why the UnLonely Project and Why Now?" https://artandhealing.org/unlonely-overview/.

Fowler, James H., and Nicholas Christakis. 2008. "Dynamic Spread of Happiness in a Large Social Network: Longitudinal Analysis over 20 Years in the Framingham Heart Study." *British Medical Journal* 337 (2338): 1–9.

Freire, Paulo, and Donald Macedo. 1987. *Reading the Word and the World*. Santa Barbara, CA: Praeger.

Galinsky, Ellen. 2010. *Mind in the Making: The Seven Essential Life Skills Every Child Needs*. New York: HarperStudio.

Gallo, Carmine. 2011. "What Makes Your Heart Sing?" *Forbes Magazine*. forbes.com/sites/carminegallo/2011/10/10/steve-jobs-what-makes-your-heart-sing/

———. 2016. *The Storyteller's Secret: From TED Speakers to Business Legends Why Some Ideas Catch On and Others Don't*. New York: St. Martin's Griffin.

Gambrell, Linda. 1996. "Creating Classrooms Cultures That Foster Reading Motivation." *The Reading Teacher* 50: 4–25.

Glenberg, Arthur, Tiana Gutierrez, Joel Levin, Sandra Japuntich, and Michael Kaschak. 2004. "Activity and Imagined Activity Can Enhance Young Children's Reading Comprehension." *Journal of Educational Psychology* 94: 424–436.

Glenberg, Arthur, Beth Jaworski, Michael Rischal, and Joel R. Levin. 2007. "What Brains Are For: Action, Meaning and Reading Comprehension." In:*Reading Comprehension Strategies: Theories, Interventions, and Technologies*, ed. D. McNamara. Mahwah, NH: Lawrence Erlbaum.

Gold, Judith and Akimi Gibson. 2001. Reading Aloud to Build Comprehension. *Reading Rockets*. readingrockets.org/article/reading-aloud-build-comprehension.

Goldberg, Gravity. 2015. *Mindsets and Moves: Strategies That Help Readers Take Charge*. Thousand Oaks, CA: Corwin.

Goodman, Yetta M. 1985. "Kidwatching: Observing Children in the Classroom." In: *Observing the Language Learner,* ed. A. Jagger and M. T. Smith-Burke, 9–18. Urbana, IL: NCTE and IRA.

Gotschall, Jonathan. 2013. *The Storytelling Animal: How Stories Make Us Human.* Boston, MA: Mariner Books.

Graves, Donald. 1983. *Writing: Teachers and Children at Work.* Portsmouth, NH: Heinemann.

Gray, Peter. 2010. "The Decline of Play and Rise in Children's Mental Disorders." *Psychology Today* [blog]. psychologytoday.com/us/blog/ freedom-learn/201001/the-decline-play-and-rise-in-childrens-mental-disorders.

Gregerson, Hal. 2018. "Better Brainstorming." *Harvard Business Review.* 64-71. https://hbr.org/2018/03/better-brainstorming

Gurdon, Meghan Cox. 2019. *The Enchanted Horse: The Miraculous Power of Reading Aloud in the Age of Distraction.* New York: Harper.

Guthrie, John R., and Nicole Humenick M. 2004. "Motivating Students to Read: Evidence for Classroom Practices That Increase Motivation and Achievement." In: *The Voice of Evidence in Reading Research,* ed. P. McCardle and V. Chhabra, 329–354. Baltimore, MD: Paul Brookes.

Hallowell, Edward. 2003. *The Childhood Roots of Sustained Happiness: Five Steps to Help Kids Create and Sustain Lifelong Joy.* New York: Ballantine Books.

Hernandez, Katherine Mills. 2018. *Activate: Deeper Learning through Movement, Talk, and Flexible Classrooms.* Portsmouth, NH: Stenhouse.

Ivey, Gay, and Karen Broaddus. 2001. "Just Plain Reading: A Survey of What Makes Students Want to Read in Middle Schools." *Reading Research Quarterly* 36: 350–377.

Jackson, Susan, and Mihaly Csikszentmihalyi. 1999. *Flow in Sports: The Keys to Optimal Experiences and Performances.* Champaign, IL: Human Kinetics Books.

Jobs, Steve. 2005. Stanford University Commencement Address. youtube.com/ watch?v=D1R-jKKp3NA

Johnson, Ned, and William Strixrud. 2018. *The Self-Driven Child: The Science and Sense of Giving Your Kids More Control over Their Lives.* New York: Viking.

Johnston, Peter. 2004. *Choice Words: How Our Language Affects Children's Learning.* Portland, ME: Stenhouse.

Juliani, A.J. 2014. *Inquiry and Innovation in the Classroom: Using 20% Time, Genius Hour, and PBL to Drive Student Success.* New York: Routledge.

Kaufman, Scott Barry. 2015. "Which Character Strengths Are Most Predictive of Well-Being." *Scientific American.* Available online at: scientificamerican.com/beautiful-minds/which-character-strengths-are-most-predictive-of-well-being/.

Keene, Ellin Oliver, and Susan Zimmerman. 2007. *Mosaic of Thought: The Power of Comprehension Strategy Instruction.* 2nd ed. Portsmouth, NH: Heinemann.

Keltner, Dacher, and Jonathan Haidt. 2003. "Approaching Awe: A Moral, Spiritual, and Aesthetic Emotion." *Cognition and Emotion* 17 (2): 297–314.

Keyes, Ralph. 2003. The *Courage to Write: How Writers Transcend Fear.* New York: Henry Holt and Company.

Klem, Adena M., and James P. Connell. 2004. "Relationships Matter: Linking Teacher Support to Student Engagement and Achievement." *Journal of School Health* 74 (7): 262–273.

Kuhl, Patricia. 2007. Is Speech Learning 'Gated' By the Social Brain? *Development Science,* 10: 110-120.

Lahey, Jessica. 2015. *The Gift of Failure: How the Best Parents Learn to Let Go So Their Children Can Succeed.* New York: Harper Paperbacks.

———. 2016. "Letting Happiness Flourish in the Classroom." *New York Times.* Available online at: well.blogs.nytimes.com/2016/03/09/happiness-in-the-classroom/.

Layne, Steven, L. 2015. *In Defense of Read Aloud: Sustaining Best Practice.* Portland, ME: Stenhouse.

Lego Foundation. 2018. "Why Play." legofoundation.com/en/why-play/.

Lyding, Linnea, Debby Zambo, and Cory Cooper Hansen. 2014. "Move It or Lose It." *Educational Leadership* 72 (2). Available online at: ascd.org/publications/educational-leadership/oct14/vol72/num02/Move-It-or-Lose-it!.aspx

Lyon, George Ella. 1999. *Where I'm From: Where Poems Come From.* Spring, TX: Absey & Co.

Meyers, Christopher. 2014. "The Apartheid of Children's Literature." *New York Times,* March 15.

Mills, Heidi. 2005. "It's All About Looking Closely and Listening Carefully." *School Talk* 11 (1): 1–2.

Mooney, Margaret, E. 1990. *Reading to, with, and by Children.* Richard C. Owen.

Mraz, Kristine, Alison Porcelli, and Cheryl Tyler. 2016. *Purposeful Play: A Teacher's Guide to Igniting Deep and Joyful Learning Across the Day*. Portsmouth, NH: Heinemann.

Nathanson, Lori, Susan E. Rivers, Lisa M. Flynn, and Marc A. Brackett. 2016. "Creating Emotionally Intelligent Schools with RULER." *Emotion Review* 8 (4): 1–6.

Neuman, Susan, Carol Copple, and Sue Bredekamp. 2000. *Learning to Read and Write: Developmentally Appropriate Practices for Young Children*. Washington, DC: National Association for the Education of Young Children.

Newkirk, Thomas. 2014. *Minds Made for Stories: How We Really Read and Write Informational and Persuasive Texts*. Portsmouth, NH: Heinemann.

Pink, Daniel. 2009. *Drive: The Surprising Truth About What Motivates Us*. New York: Riverhead Books.

Resnick, Lauren, Sarah Michaels, and Catherine O'Connor. 2008. "Deliberative Discourse Idealized and Realized: Accountable Talk in the Classroom and in Civic Life." *Studies in Philosophy and Education* 27 (4): 283–297.

Routman, Regie. 2000. *Conversations: Strategies for Teaching, Learning, and Evaluating*. Portsmouth, NH: Heinemann.

Rubin, Gretchen. 2013. *Better Than Before: What I Learned About Making and Breaking Habits—To Sleep More, Quit Sugar, Procrastinate Less, and Generally Build a Happier Life*. Portland, OR: Broadway Books.

Scholastic. 2019. *Kids and Family Reading Report: The Rise of Read-Aloud*. New York: Scholastic. Available online at http://www.scholastic.com/readingreport/.

Seidel, Aly. 2014. "The Teacher Dropout Crisis." *National Public Radio*. Available online at: npr.org/sections/ed/2014/07/18/332343240/the-teacher-dropout-crisis.

Seligman, Martin. 2012. *Flourish: A Visionary New Understanding of Happiness and Well-Being*. New York: Atria Books.

Seligman, Martin E. P., Randal M. Ernst, Jane Gillham, Karen Reivich, and Mark Linkins. 2009. "Positive Education: Positive Psychology and Classroom Interventions." *Oxford Review of Education* 35: 293–311.

Seppala, Emma. 2017. *The Happiness Track: How to Apply the Science of Happiness to Accelerate Your Success*. New York: HarperOne.

Smith, Suzanne F. 2019. *The Writing Shop: Putting "Shop" Back in Writing Workshop*. Boston: Brill Sense.

Sullivan, Amie, K., and Harold R. Strang. 2002. "Bibliotherapy in the Classroom: Using Literature to Promote the Development of Emotional Intelligence." *Childhood Education* 792: 74–80.

Unicef Office of Research. 2007. *Child Well-Being in Rich Countries*. Unicef Office of Research. https://www.unicef-irc.org/publications/pdf/rc11_eng.pdf.

Wiking, Meik. 2017. *The Little Book of Hygge: Danish Secrets to Happy Living*. New York: William Morrow.

Wilkinson, Ian A. G., and Eun Hye Son. 2011. "A Dialogic Turn in Research on Learning and Teaching to Comprehend." In: *Handbook of Reading Research*: Volume IV, ed. M. L. Kamil, P. B. Rosenthal, P. D. Pearson, and R. Barr, 359–387. New York: Routledge.

Yaffe, Deborah. 2018. "Bye, Bye, Loneliness." *Princeton Alumni Weekly*. https://paw.princeton.edu/article/bye-bye-loneliness

INDEX